Faith in Christ Is Eternal Life

Faith in Christ <u>Is</u> Eternal Life

Understanding God's Free Grace

How to know that you are saved

by

Matthew Correll

Wonderment
Simplicity
Grace
Love
Joy

†

Faith in Christ Is Eternal Life
Understanding God's Free Grace

Fulfillment Press
PO Box 871607
Canton, Michigan 48187

Version: 2
FIC-text 2009-04-01
FIC-cover 2009-04-01

Printed in the United States of America

ISBN 978-0-9820920-1-9

Special Thanks to:

Arianna for inspiring some of the chapters.

David Cray for evocative editing.

John Correll for printing and other editorial advice.

Bob Wilkin, Robert Dean and Zane Hodges for online tutorship.

And, of course: Jesus Christ, God the Father and the Holy Spirit!

Contents

Foreword

This is a compilation of free grace theology from my books: *O.S.A.S, Sola Fide, Free Not Cheap, Secure in Christ* and *Faith Needs No Work*. It is a defense of the true biblical gospel of Jesus Christ our Lord and is a full-orbed refutation of Lordship salvation and other manmade systems of theology! I chose this title for the sake of giving the gospel in the entitlement before even endeavoring into the book.

This book is also a theological guide in understanding salvation, the errors of Lordship Salvation, Arminianism and Calvinism. It is a multifaceted venture into free grace theology for both the layman and the doctrinaire scholar.

But in case you are wondering...

WHAT IS LORDSHIP SALVATION?

It is the idea that simple faith in Christ is not enough for salvation and that we must do something extra, i.e., making Christ Lord of our lives in persistent obedience. It misrepresents repentance and re-qualifies saving faith. It leaves no assurance of salvation.

WHAT IS ARMINIANISM?

It's a flawed system that overvalues man's freewill insofar that they deem that man can lose his salvation due to sin, renunciation, backsliding, ... etc.

WHAT IS CALVINISM?

It's another flawed system that evokes that man can't lose his salvation, but he can prove to have never really possessed it if he does not persevere to the end. It also removes freewill and over-emphasizes the fatalistic sovereignty of God grace.

WHAT IS FREE GRACE THEOLOGY?

It's the idea that God saves man freely, apart from anything man can do by his own efforts. Grace: literally means, the unmerited favor of God. Salvation is a free gift. All man has to do is to receive it by believing. (John 1:12.) Faith is non-meritorious and simply a response to God's offer of eternal life.

I sincerely hope that the reader will enjoy this book and grow in grace as well — 2 Peter 3:18.

Anonymous Free Grace Quotes

To semantically smuggle obedience into the definition of saving faith is linguistic subterfuge.

* * *

Lordship salvation makes it so the lost can't be saved and the saved can't have assurance!

* * *

Faith that examines itself is unbelief.

* * *

We must not direct one lens of the telescope of faith to look at the historical "Done" of the past, and a second lens to look at some vague, experiential "Do" of the future. The only worthy object of our attention is Jesus Christ alone, not ourselves.

* * *

The evangelist who insists that the ungodly must obey the supernatural request to fully submit to the Lordship of Christ in order to be saved is asking the unregenerate to fulfill a command that is the greatest challenge for even the most mature believer in Christ to obey!

* * *

If a person just thinks of repentance as turning from sinful practices, repentance becomes a good work that a person does.

This kind of repentance is not necessary for salvation for two reasons. First, this is not how the gospel preachers in the New Testament used the word, as one can see from the meaning of the Greek word metanoia. Second, other Scriptures make it clear that good works, including turning from sin, have no part in justification (e.g., Eph. 2:8–9). God does not save us because of what we do for Him but because of what He has done for us in Christ.

* * *

We believe, also, that our redemption has been accomplished solely by the blood of our Lord Jesus Christ, who was made to be sin and was made a curse for us, dying in our place and stead; and that no repentance, no feeling, no faith, no good resolutions, no sincere efforts, no submission to the rules and regulations of any church, nor all the churches that have existed since the days of the Apostles can add in the very least degree to the value of the blood, or to the merit of the finished work of Jesus Christ.

* * *

You don't need to spend countless hours worrying over whether or not you have enough faith. If you have "JUST ENOUGH" faith to "CALL UPON THE NAME OF THE LORD", that's all the faith you need to be saved. Either you "believe" on the Lord Jesus, or you don't. I believe!

* * *

The Apostle Paul never promoted holy living as a means to bring lost sinners to true justification and eternal life. He taught continually, as did all the Apostles, that God's only means of saving sinners is through the preaching of the Gospel of salvation conditioned on Christ's righteousness ALONE.

* * *

If we could forsake our sins in order to be saved, we'd either need no Saviour, become our own Saviour or at best reduce the Saviourship of Christ to an unnecessary pedestrian triviality. Such a nonsensical stance would be a prodigious sin, yet to be forsaken!

* * *

Indeed, no more fitting label may be applied to the entire Arminian system than that of a damning lie. As "a corrupt tree cannot bring forth good fruit" (Matthew 7:18), many of the ethical problems which plague modern Evangelicalism can be traced right back to the man-centered theology of Arminianism, which reduces God to a sappy, enfeebled geriatric who is ever fearful of "coming on too strong." It is no wonder that such a god fails to stir up a deep reverence and worship within the hearts of his devotees..."

* * *

Not trusting Christ solely for salvation leads to hell; Lordship Salvation just makes the pathway to hell clearer and more accessible.

* * *

"The Gospel is not a call to repentance, or to amendment of our ways, to make restitution for past sins, or to promise to do better in the future. These things are proper in their place, but they do not constitute the Gospel; for the Gospel is not good advice to be obeyed, it is good news to be believed. Do not make the mistake then of thinking that the Gospel is a call to duty or a call to reformation, a call to better your condition, to behave yourself in a more perfect way than you have been doing in the past... Nor is the Gospel a demand that you give up the world, that you give up your sins, that you break off bad habits, and try to cultivate good ones. You may do all these things, and yet never believe the Gospel and consequently never be saved at all."

* * *

A worldly Christian is focused on and content in sin, a spiritual Christian is not, yet he is still customarily seduced by it.

* * *

If we had to repent, stop sinning, turn from sins, forsake our sins, be willing to stop sinning, or do anything else in order to be saved other than just placing faith/trust in Christ, then it wouldn't matter if God is good, it would only matter if WE were good. Such a notion is antithetical to the gospel and blasphemous!

* * *

Religion or Lordship Salvation leads to pride: 'I did it' or despair: 'I can't do it!' It never leads to Jesus!

* * *

Making Christ Lord of my life is not about slavish acquiescence to a bunch of incomprehensible rules, it's more about having a provider, a sustainer, someone to quarterback my decisions and someone who answers my prayers in abundance, someone to rely upon in trying times. Sure He is my Lord, but not in the sense of master and slave, but like Father and son.

* * *

The truth is that we have churches all across America filled with Christians who are sitting on the premises instead of standing on the promises.

~ 1 ~

The Gift of God

Romans 3:24 (NAS) — *Being justified as a gift by His grace through the redemption which is in Christ Jesus.*

Salvation is a gift from God. Lordship Salvation fails to see this. They make salvation more of a quid pro quo. You do for God and He'll do for you. But the Bible doesn't teach this. Salvation is simple. So is receiving a gift. Heretics on the gospel have taken away the easiness and readiness of receiving a gift, which is what salvation is. How hard is it to receive a gift? Ask any child.

If someone offered you a gift, receiving it would be so simple that the only thing that could trammel such a reception would be the lack of anticipation or an aversion to the gift itself. But if the gift was desirable, which salvation, or everlasting life in heaven indubitably should be—then how hard could it be to accept a gift from God? That is exactly what salvation is—a free gift!

Here is a list of scriptures in biblical order that explain more about this marvelous gift of God.

Proverbs 17:8 — *A gift is as a precious stone in the eyes of him that hath it: whithersoever it turneth, it prospereth.*

Gifts are precious. No one can deny this.

But not all gifts from God are referring to salvation.

Ecclesiastes 3:13 — *And also that every man should eat and drink, and enjoy the good of all his labour, it is the gift of God.*

Ecclesiastes 5:19 — *Every man also to whom God hath given riches and wealth, and hath given him power to eat thereof, and to take his portion, and to rejoice in his labour; this is the gift of God.*

Gifts come in many forms.

Matthew 7:11 — *If ye then, being evil, know how to give good gifts unto your children, how much more shall your Father which is in heaven give good things to them that ask him?*

But salvation is undeniably a gift from God.

John 4:10 — *Jesus answered and said unto her, If thou knewest the gift of God, and who it is that saith to thee, Give me to drink; thou wouldest have asked of him, and he would have given thee living water.*

Although salvation is a free gift from God, God bestows other gifts as well, I.e., the Holy Spirit.

Acts 2:38 – *Then Peter said unto them, Repent, and be baptized every one of you in the name of Jesus Christ for the remission of sins, and ye shall receive the gift of the Holy Ghost.*

Some people in the Bible tried to purchase the Holy Spirit, but this is not possible. No gift can be purchased monetarily.

Acts 8:20 — *But Peter said unto him, Thy money perish with thee, because thou hast thought that the gift of God may be purchased with money.*

Salvation is unquestionably a gift according to scripture.

Acts 11:17 — *Forasmuch then as God gave them the like gift as he did unto us, who believed on the Lord Jesus Christ; what was I, that I could withstand God?*

The Bible is clear that not all gifts are about salvation. Just as the Holy Spirit is a gift so are spiritual gifts.

Romans 1:11 — *For I long to see you, that I may impart unto you some spiritual gift, to the end ye may be established.*

But the best understanding of God's gift is reified in the gift of salvation. Look how many times the word gift appears in these scriptures.

Romans 5:15–18 — *But not as the offence, so also is the free gift. For if through the offence of one many be dead, much more the grace of God, and the gift by grace, which is by one man, Jesus Christ, hath abounded unto many. And not as it was by one that sinned, so is the gift: for the judgment was by one to condemnation, but the free gift is of many offences unto justification. For if by one man's offence death reigned by one; much more they which receive abundance of grace and of the gift of righteousness shall reign in life by one, Jesus Christ. Therefore as by the offence of one judgment came upon all men to condemnation; even so by the righteousness of one the free gift came upon all men unto justification of life.*

Salvation is the most precious gift God offers to sinners.

Romans 6:23 — *For the wages of sin is death; but the gift of God is eternal life through Jesus Christ our Lord.*

God's gift can't be revoked. Salvation can't be lost. Nor can it be forfeited. This scripture alone refutes any such heretical doctrine!

Romans 11:29 — *For the gifts and calling of God are without repentance.*

I'll say it again. The most precious promise in scripture is that salvation is a free gift!

Ephesians 2:8 — *For by grace are ye saved through faith; and that not of yourselves: it is the gift of God.*

Hebrews 6:4 — *For it is impossible for those who were once enlightened, and have tasted of the heavenly gift, and were made partakers of the Holy Ghost.*

James 1:17 — *Every good gift and every perfect gift is from above, and cometh down from the Father of lights, with whom is no variableness, neither shadow of turning.*

1 Peter 4:10 — *As every man hath received the gift, even so minister the same one to another, as good stewards of the manifold grace of God.*

2 Corinthians 9:15 — *Thanks be unto God for his unspeakable gift.*

Faith needs no work!

~ 2 ~

All of Grace

Christians talk about the fact that we are saved by grace and even justified by grace, but we must never forget that every aspect and corollary of salvation is also by God's free grace. This is the good news.

SALVATION IS BY GRACE

Acts 15:11 — *But we believe that through the <u>grace</u> of the LORD Jesus Christ we shall be <u>saved</u>, even as they.*

Ephesians 2:8 — *For by <u>grace</u> are ye <u>saved</u> through faith; and that not of yourselves: it is the gift of God.*

REDEMPTION IS BY GRACE

Ephesians 1:7 — *In whom we have <u>redemption</u> through his blood, the forgiveness of sins, according to the riches of his <u>grace</u>.*

JUSTIFICATION IS BY GRACE

Romans 3:24 — *Being <u>justified</u> freely by his <u>grace</u> through the redemption that is in Christ Jesus.*

OUR CALLING IS BY GRACE

Galatians 1:15 — *But when it pleased God, who separated me from my mother's womb, and <u>called</u> me by his <u>grace</u>.*

ELECTION IS BY GRACE

Romans 11:5 — *Even so then at this present time also there is a remnant according to the <u>election</u> of <u>grace</u>.*

GLORIFICATION IS BY GRACE

2 Thessalonians 1:12 — *That the name of our Lord Jesus Christ may be <u>glorified</u> in you, and ye in him, according to the <u>grace</u> of our God and the Lord Jesus Christ.*

OUR WORKS ARE BY GRACE

1 Corinthians 15:10 — *But by the grace of God I am what I am: and his grace which was bestowed upon me was not in vain; but I <u>laboured</u> more abundantly than they all: yet not I, but the <u>grace</u> of God which was with me.*

THE GOSPEL IS BY GRACE

Acts 20:24 — *But none of these things move me, neither count I my life dear unto myself, so that I might finish my course with joy, and the ministry, which I have received of the Lord Jesus, to testify the <u>gospel</u> of the <u>grace</u> of God.*

THE ABRAHAMIC PROMISE IS BY GRACE

Romans 4:16 — *Therefore it is of faith, that it might be by <u>grace</u>; to the end the <u>promise</u> might be sure to all the seed; not to that only which is of the law, but to that also which is of the faith of Abraham; who is the father of us all.*

FORGIVENESS IS BY GRACE

Ephesians 1:7 — *In whom we have redemption through his blood, the <u>forgiveness</u> of sins, according to the riches of his <u>grace</u>.*

PEACE IS BY GRACE

Galatians 1:3 — *Grace be to you and peace from God the Father, and from our Lord Jesus Christ.*

Free Not Cheap!

When Jesus therefore had received the vinegar, he said, It is finished: and he bowed his head, and gave up the ghost. — John 19:30.

~ 3 ~

The Finished Work of Christ
(All Sins Are Future Sins)

So many Christians will say that Christ died only for your past sins. This is a seemingly failsafe way of promoting Arminianism and even some strange breeds of Lordship Salvation. Hmm, if Christ only died for your sins past then there must be something we must do to cover our present and future sins. This is just rhetorical trickery. Christ died for all your sins. Past, present, future.

Colossians 2:13 — *And you, being dead in your sins and the uncircumcision of your flesh, hath he quickened together with him, having forgiven you all trespasses.*

If He died for only your past sins, but not your future sins, why does the scripture say that we have been forgiven all trespasses? It makes no sense!

The Bible says that when we are justified, we are justified from all things.

Acts 13:39 — *And by him all that believe are justified from all things, from which ye could not be justified by the law of Moses.*

If only your past sins were forgiven then how could this verse be true?

23

It would have to be read: And by him all that believe are justified from <u>some things</u> or <u>past things</u>, from which ye could not be justified by the law of Moses.

All means all and that's all, all means! Period. If Christ only died for our past sins nobody would have a conclusive or insightful answer as to how our present and future sins are to be covered. Ritual sacrifice, periodic confession, Christ redying, sinless perfection. The conclusion is unknowable, preposterous and unbiblical. If one sacrifice weren't enough then Christ would have to die again and again and again. This is absurd.

Romans 6:10 — *For in that he died, he died unto sin <u>once</u>: but in that he liveth, he liveth unto God.*

All your sins are future sins considering that Christ died before you were born.

John 10:14–17 — *I am the good shepherd, and know my sheep, and am known of mine. As the Father knoweth me, even so know I the Father: and I lay down my life for the sheep. And other sheep I have, which are not of this fold: them also I must bring, and they shall hear my voice; and there shall be one fold, and one shepherd. Therefore doth my Father love me, because I lay down my life, that I might take it again.*

Take a close look at verse 16.

John 10:16 — *And <u>other sheep</u> I have, which are not of this fold: them also I must bring, and they shall hear my voice; and there shall be one fold, and one shepherd.*

The other sheep is referring to us, ... Christians of the future. It wasn't referring to Christians back in the Bible times that lived in a foreign country away from Christ's local herd. No. Anyone who has believed on Christ for salvation was part of the fold. The fact that this verse says that there are other sheep that are not of this fold means that the other sheep are the ones not born yet—us—the Christians of today. This is proof that all our sins are future and forgiven. Christ promises to bring all believers into heaven with Him.

Only heretics say such things like: Christ only died for your past sins. Such people are only saying this because they want this to be true. Obviously, they either aren't saved, or they don't want to go to heaven, or they want to atone for their present and future sins in another manner. Or they just arrogantly think that they won't or don't sin anymore. This is as close to blasphemy as one can come to committing!

All your sins are future sins unless you historically predated Christ. And none of you reading this have.

To suggest that Christ only died for your past sins is implying that the job of sacrificial atonement wasn't finished.

Here is an exegesis on John 19:28–30.

John 19:28 — *After this, Jesus knowing that all things were now accomplished, that the scripture might be fulfilled, saith, I thirst.*

29 — *Now there was set a vessel full of vinegar: and they filled a spunge with vinegar, and put it upon hyssop, and put it to his mouth.*

30 — *When Jesus therefore had received the vinegar, he said, It is finished: and he bowed his head, and gave up the ghost.*

"It is finished" in Greek is Tetelastai, which means "paid in full."

Christ is the author and finisher of our faith. (Hebrews 12:2.)

Christ did it all. There is nothing for us to do but believe. Let's break "Tetelastai" down. In Greek it is in the perfect tense. That describes an action that has taken place in the past, once and for all, which needs not to be repeated and remains true forevermore.

The Greek voice is passive which represents the subject as being the recipient of the action.

I.e., Christ died for sinners. The sinner receives Christ. We received the action of Christ through faith. The Greek mood is infinitive. The infinitive mood is used to indicate the purpose or goal of the action or state. In this case, "it is finished" represents what Christ did for us. We can't add or subtract anything from this once we are saved. In other words, nothing can alter our salvation.

If there were any additional works to be done in association to the finished work of Christ, they too would have to be done before the world began.

Hebrews 4:3 — *For we which have believed do enter into rest, as he said, As I have sworn in my wrath, if they shall enter into my rest: although the works were finished from the foundation of the world.*

This truth should embolden our faith in Christ!

Faith needs no work.

~ 4 ~

Position in Christ

It is important to know your position in Christ. As believers we are more than just saved. We are now and forevermore positioned in Christ. This should give us hope and certainty that we are going to heaven. Lordship Salvation proponents don't like nor do they understand the position of the believer. The position is so permanent that it guarantees our eternal life. Look at the connection between our position and our guaranteed impending abode in heaven.

2 Timothy 2:11 — *It is a faithful saying: For if we be dead with him, we shall also live with him.*

'Dead' in Greek is: Sunapothenesko, which means literally to be in company or association with. This is our position in Christ. Check your concordance and see for yourself. We are positionally secure in Christ. The objectors of this doctrine can only mendaciously say that this position isn't permanent and that there is something we can do—like some sin—to de-position us. How fallacious is their argument. Look at our position: Dead with him. Now read the verse again. For if we be dead with him (positionally) we shall also live with him!

Living with Christ means being with Him in heaven. Here's more proof that our position in Christ promises us heaven.

1 Corinthians 1:30 — *But of him are ye in Christ Jesus, who of God is made unto us wisdom, and righteousness, and sanctification, and redemption.*

"Redemption" — that's talking about heaven for certainly we haven't physically been redeemed in this life. The objectors to eternal security will have an impossible job rebutting this verse. But how do I know that simple faith is all it takes to secure our position in Christ?

Galatians 3:26 — *For ye are all the children of God (positionally) by faith in Christ Jesus.*

Another positional terminology is "Crucified." The thieves on the cross were literally crucified with Christ but this verse is speaking figuratively, positionally.

Galatians 2:20 — *I am crucified with Christ: nevertheless I live; yet not I, but Christ liveth in me: and the life which I now live in the flesh I live by the faith of the Son of God, who loved me, and gave himself for me.*

'Crucified' in Greek is Sustauroo, which means the same thing as Sunapothenesko. To be associated with. This is positional terminology,

Romans 8:1, 1 Corinthians 1:30 and 2 Corinthians 5:17 all refer to being "in Christ." This too is about our position in Christ.

Romans 6, is all about our position versus our experience.

Paul states our position in verse 3 and then tells us how we ought to behave because of our position.

Here I will show you the difference between our position and our experience.

Romans 6:1–11 says the following.

Romans 6:1 — *What shall we say then? Shall we continue in sin, that grace may abound?*

2 — *God forbid. How shall we, that are dead to sin, live any longer therein?*

3 — *Know ye not, that so many of us as were baptized into Jesus Christ (position) were baptized into his death (position)?*

4 — *Therefore we are buried with him by baptism into death: (position) that like as Christ was raised up from the dead by the glory of the Father, even so we also should (experience) walk in newness of life.*

Notice the word "should," not must! Lordship Salvation proponents hate this!

5 — *For if we have been planted together in the likeness of his death, (position) we shall be also in the likeness of his resurrection. (Position).*

6 — *Knowing this, that our old man is crucified with him, (position) that the body of sin might be destroyed, that henceforth we should not serve sin. (Experience.)*

7 — *For he that is dead is freed from sin.*

8 — *Now if we be dead with Christ, (position) we believe that we shall also live with him. (Position.)*

9 — *Knowing that Christ being raised from the dead dieth no more; death hath no more dominion over him.*

10 — *For in that he died, he died unto sin once: but in that he liveth, he liveth unto God.*

11 — *Likewise reckon ye also yourselves to be dead indeed unto sin, but alive unto God through Jesus Christ our Lord.*

Colossians 3:1–3 is also referring to our position versus our experience.

Colossians 3:1–3 says the following.

Colossians 3:1 — *If ye then be risen with Christ, (position) seek those things which are above, (experience) where Christ sitteth on the right hand of God.*

2 — *Set your affection on things above, not on things on the earth. (Experience.)*

3 — *For ye are dead, (position) and your life is hid (position) with Christ in God.*

* * *

The "positional" terminology is this.

"In." Romans 8:1.

"Crucified." Galatians 2:20.

"Planted." Romans 6:5.

"Baptized." Romans 6:3.

"Buried." Colossians 2:12.

"Dead." 2 Timothy 2:11.

"Complete." Colossians 2:10.

"Hid." Colossians 3:3.

"Sanctified." 1 Corinthians 1:2.

"Asleep." 1 Corinthians 15:18.

"Risen." Colossians 3:1.

Our position in Christ has nothing to do with our experience as believers. I.e., our spiritual walk. The position is an established and settled fact.

Ephesians 1:5 — *Having predestinated us unto the adoption of children by Jesus Christ to himself, according to the good pleasure of his will.*

No sin or series of sins can alter, change or negate our position in Christ, despite what any Arminian or Lordship Salvationist may say. Those who think that salvation can be lost don't understand that their position in Christ is real and promises them heaven.

1 Thessalonians 5:23 — *And the very God of peace sanctify you wholly; and I pray God your whole spirit and soul and body be preserved blameless unto the coming of our Lord Jesus Christ.*

Our position in Christ also promises us the Holy Spirit.

John 14:16 — *And I will pray the Father, and he shall give you another Comforter, that he may abide with you for ever.*

The Holy Spirit is our comforter and will be with us forever.

That proves that our position in Christ can't be withdrawn or undone.

Faith needs no work.

For the gifts and calling of God are without repentance. — Romans 11:29.

~ 5 ~

GiveSalvationBackism
(A Response to the Arminian Heresy)

Free Grace theology highly refutes the idea that salvation can be forfeited either by volition or by sin, so I felt it was of necessary importance to include a refutation of what I have duly dubbed: givesalvationbackism.

THE CONCERNS ABOUT THIS DOCTRINE

- It's a distortion of the true gospel.

- It's not a side issue.

- It's logically inconsistent.

- It's dishonest.

- It's unbiblical.

- It's an issue that is inevitably answered with: "Now you're just talking semantics."

- It has evangelistic problems.

I will try to present this as logically, irenically and non-litigiously as possible. (This chapter before editing it into this book was a letter I wrote to someone on the topic of Arminianism.)

The Letter:

Please read this entirely, objectively and openly before developing any rebuttal. The rest of this chapter is the letter in entirety.

The O.S.A.S. (Once saved always saved) issue is NOT a side issue! The position you take determines whether or not the true gospel is being understood. Now you can preach the gospel either way but you can't fully understand it without embracing eternal security. The ones on the you-can-give-your-salvation-back side have distorted the gospel unwittingly.

Think about it. Salvation is either by the sufficiency of Christ or it is not. Salvation is simply placing your trust in Christ and nothing else. If man could do anything to merit salvation, then Christ is out of the picture. If man could do anything to jettison his salvation, then the permanency of Christ's finished work is negated totally. Man doesn't do anything to earn salvation, keep salvation or lose salvation. For the gifts and calling of God are irrevocable.

Scripture says that Christ died for all your sins.

Colossians 2:13 — *And you, being dead in your sins and the uncircumcision of your flesh, hath he quickened together with him, having forgiven you all trespasses.*

It's illogical to think that you can give salvation back without concluding that a person's post-forfeiture sins are not covered. You'd have to either reverse the crucifixion, which in turn would necessitate Christ dying all over again or find some other modality of atonement. The Bible is teetotal against this. One is left surmising that there are sins (post-forfeiture) that Christ somehow couldn't, wouldn't or didn't cover when He died for us. The real question is whether Christ is sufficient or not. The givesalvation-backists are incognizantly saying no!

It is a known fact that both sides of this argument can be proof-texted by scripture. But you can't have both. Scripture either says one thing or the other—it can't contradict. The answer to the OSAS question needs to be resolute. If it leaves necessary questions, then the answer is anything but resolute. This whole: "You can't lose salvation but you can give it back is not even an answer.

It is a copout. A contradiction. It's synonymous to saying "yes" and "no". <u>CAN'T</u> lose it, <u>CAN</u> give it back? You can't have two antithetical terms coming from the same statement and claim resolution.

Which one is it? Isn't losing it the same thing as giving it back if the outcome is tantamount in both situations? This is when the contrived rejoinder will inevitably come: "Now you're just talking semantics." Well is that answering the question? No! It is copout number 2. It would be like me asking, "what's two plus two?" And then someone answering with: "a math problem." "Sure, it's a math problem, but you haven't numerically answered it."

C. I. Scofield said that a "verily" cannot be contradicted by an "if."

When Jesus says verily, verily I say unto you he that believeth on me hath everlasting life; he meant just that. The whole givesalvationbackistic theory would implant some "ifs" into your soteriology.

One problem with Arminian doctrine is that it is a dishonest doctrine.

Imagine someone coming up to one of the Arminian ministers or teachers with the following problem.

John Doe: "I've been saved by faith in Christ but I feel like I might have given my salvation back. What should I do?"

The church's response would either be: "Nothing. I don't know. Or they would have to dishonestly say that salvific loss was not possible. They would have to pull out an eternal security verse to give any consolation."

See the inconsistency.

Now, this church could stick to its guns and say, "We don't think you gave your salvation back. Or you're still saved, you'd have to REALLY want to give it back or make a pledge against God and we don't think that you did that."

You see these speculative responses wouldn't be much consolation because the consoler doesn't know why this sorrowful person thought he gave his salvation back? It could've been anger or a vocal pledge or who knows maybe at the time he REALLY wanted to give it back. The givesalvationbackism would be left saying one of two things.

"Yes you did give it back, you're doomed! Go shoot yourself so that hell doesn't become worse due to future sins..."

Or.

"Uhhh. You need to find someone who believes in eternal security (like a Baptist) so that you feel like you're saved again and get some solace.

Both responses are lame and dishonest!

We can at least agree on that point.

Eternal security is nonnegotiable.

Givesalvationbackism is offensive in that it causes people to subconsciously infer that they have given their salvation back. I have two friends that were saved, but are now living in darkness because they both were convinced that they had given their salvation back. The teaching of eternal security might have prevented this!

The reason we shouldn't teach givesalvationbackism is because the power of suggestion may eventuate into self-actualization at least epistemically.

There is a psychological fact that what you tell someone becomes subjectively true because of suggestion. When I was young I used to boss my sisters around all the time and they slavishly acquiesced without question or defiance, until my dad suggested, not enjoined, but suggested that kids don't listen to kids. I tried to boss my sister around thereafter and she stopped obeying and responded with: "kids don't listen to kids."

This is the power of suggestion. If you implant the notion into someone's mind that they can give their salvation back, you've just made it possible for Satan to convince them that they have or will. Your own doctrine damns you if you are correct. According to Hebrews once a givesalvationbackist gives his salvation back he can't be resaved. That's called one-shot soteriology and is double heresy.

This doctrine is satanic and needs to be rejected outright.

Some may be thinking that the Bible supports the idea that you can give your salvation back. It doesn't and if it did, then God would be the author of doubts and confusion.

"Can I lose salvation?"

"Can I give it back?"

"Have I given it back?"

"What if I give it back when I become senile."

"What if I've given it back already and don't realize it."

"If I do give my salvation back is it irreversible?"

"Can scripture support both sides of this argument?"

"What if my friend gives his salvation back?"

"What?!"

"Huh!!!"

What is all this?

CONFUSION!

1 Corinthians 14:33 — *For God is not the author of confusion, but of peace, as in all churches of the saints.*

God can set you free from this heresy!

If you still think this is a side issue remember that a side issue unresolved can lead to confusion and apostasy!

I hypothetically proposed that salvation could be given back at a Bible study and immediately someone questioned if they were still saved. This doctrine stirs doubts with alacrity!

You would have to be deluded to not at least see the inherent problems with this position in this debate.

You should've said that you guys don't debate this, but instead you took the side that fosters the debate instead of just being noncommittal. Saying that you can't lose salvation but you can give it back is not being noncommittal, it is simply saying that salvation can in fact be lost but masquerading such a statement with a subtle but deceptive assertion that tacitly says that: yes salvation really can be lost by man's volition!

This is why I will not, and no Christian should, tolerate such a disastrous teaching!

Free Not Cheap!

~ 6 ~

Born of God
"Christians don't sin," Refuted

1 John 5:18 — *We know that whosoever is born of God sinneth not; but he that is begotten of God keepeth himself, and that wicked one toucheth him not.*

So many self-righteous, deceived Christians will use this verse to give honest, sinful Christians a migraine and a guilt complex. But are they interpreting this scripture correctly when they suggest that true believers no longer sin?

No. Look at 1 John 5:21 — *Little children, keep yourselves from idols. Amen.*

This is the last verse in John's first epistle. Why on earth would John be encouraging his readers to keep from idols, which is a sin by the way, when three verses prior to this he is suggesting that true Christians don't sin at all? That would be like me saying that my kids have no ability to do somersaults whatsoever but then, uncannily, I plead with them not to do them as if they had the ability. It just doesn't make any sense.

Declaring that Christians don't sin but then urging them not to commit the sin of idolatry is nonsensical and absurd. Perhaps this "sinneth not theory" is just that a theory. A wrongful theory.

When a person is born again by simple faith, it is not their flesh that has been born again. If that were the case, then yes, they would in fact sinneth not. But it is the spirit that is born again.

John 3:5 — *Jesus answered, Verily, verily, I say unto thee, Except a man be born of water and of the Spirit, he cannot enter into the kingdom of God.*

The spirit is born of God and doesn't sin at all. You as a Christian may sin 100 times a day but the spirit, which is born of God, didn't and doesn't sin at all.

"Christians don't practice sin," refuted!

Some will say that this is just referring to practicing sin, sinning habitually. They will say that this verse is not saying that a Christian will not sin at all but that they will not make a practice of sin. That's also incorrect.

Take a look at.

1 John 3:9 — *Whosoever is born of God doth not commit sin; for his seed remaineth in him: and he cannot sin, because he is born of God.*

They look the word commit up in their concordance to back this up.

This verse is saying that those who are born of God don't practice sin but it is also saying that those born of God don't sin in the absolute. But keep in mind that it is the spirit that is not sinning, never the flesh.

1 John 3:9 — *Whosoever is born of God doth not <u>commit sin</u>; for his seed remaineth in him: and he cannot sin, because he is born of God.*

The first part says commit or "practice," but the latter part says <u>cannot</u> in the absolute. Compare this to 1 John 1:8, 10.

1 John 1:8 — *If we say that we have no sin, we deceive ourselves, and the truth is not in us.*

This is talking about those who deny the doctrine of original sin. Have no sin, singular is another way of saying they have no sin nature otherwise it would have to say <u>sins</u>. If a person didn't think that they sinned, he would have pluralized his assertion by saying "I have no sins." But denying original sin would be left in the singular tense. Compare this to:

John 1:29 — *The next day John seeth Jesus coming unto him, and saith, Behold the Lamb of God, which taketh away the sin of the world.*

Jesus came to pay the penalty for our sins and our <u>sin</u> nature, ... singular.

1 John 1:10, is referring to individual acts of sins.

If we say that we have not sinned, we make him a liar, and his word is not in us.

This applies even to those that say that they don't practice sin, they make him a liar and the truth is not in them.

The idea of a Christian not sinning and not practicing sin is not found in these verses anywhere.

Nobody stops sinning.

Nobody stops practicing sin.

Nobody fully overcomes sin in this life.

Some may say that you must overcome the world in order to be saved, they imply that this means overcoming sin but let's look at what the "overcomer" verses say.

"Overcome sin" is not even found in the Bible.

1 John 5:4–5 — *For whatsoever is born of God overcometh the world: and this is the victory that overcometh the world, even our faith.*

Once again we are talking about being born of God. But how is one born of God; how does one overcome the world? Read on in verse 5...

Who is he that overcometh the world, but he that <u>believeth</u> that Jesus is the Son of God?

We are saved by faith alone. Don't let these confusing verses scare you and don't let the disgusting pride of those who misinterpret them fool you! Anyone who says that Christians don't sin or practice sins is simply full of pride and arrogance, he doesn't understand the gospel and furthermore wants no one else to go to heaven. His warped theology actually wants the gateway to heaven to be as narrow as his knowledge of the scriptures, which is pitiable.

We are Secure in Christ!

~ 7 ~

Salvation Is of the Lord

Psalm 3:8 — *Salvation belongeth unto the LORD: thy blessing is upon thy people. Selah.*

When man is saved, it is an act of God. We can't do anything to save ourselves. We must fall upon the saving arms of Jesus. Rely on Him and Him alone for salvation. Scripture is clear that God saves us and we can't by any means save ourselves. This gut-wrenches Lordship Salvation. It strikes it below the belt with a cattleprod.

Lordship Salvation must die! If we are to ever appreciate what God has done for us when He saved us we must give Him all the credit. Salvation is of the Lord.

Jonah 2:9 — *But I will sacrifice unto thee with the voice of thanksgiving; I will pay that that I have vowed. Salvation is of the LORD.*

This means that salvation is something God does. It has nothing to do with us. We need to stop trying to take credit for our salvation. Romans 4:2, Ephesians 2:8–9.

Salvation is an act of God. He does it completely. All we have to do is trust in Jesus by believing the gospel.

Psalm 68:20 — *He that is our God is the God of salvation; and unto GOD the Lord belong the issues from death.*

He is the God of our salvation. Lordship salvation doesn't quite get this. They say that we must make God Lord of our lives by our own good works. Such an endeavor is really us making ourselves Lord, which is heresy! God gives us salvation. It is His!

Psalm 65:5 — *By terrible things in righteousness wilt thou answer us, O God of our salvation; who art the confidence of all the ends of the earth, and of them that are afar off upon the sea.*

David knew this. He was no Lordship Salvationist. He asked God to save him. He didn't say to God, "Look at how good I am. I'm trying to save myself. No, he asked God to save him.

Psalm 69:1 — *Save me, O God; for the waters are come in unto my soul.*

Notice it says: "save me O God." It doesn't say: what can I do to save myself?

We cannot save ourselves; so salvation has to be of the Lord. He sent His son to die for us. He didn't send us to die for our sins, which is what Lordship Salvation implicitly evokes in their harsh messages of repent and deny yourselves. The only thing a person must deny is the heretical teaching of Lordship Salvation and works. We must deny the idea that we can save ourselves with our own good deeds. Salvation is of the Lord. Why ask God to save us if we think that we can save ourselves? It's foolish!

Exodus 14:13 — *And Moses said unto the people, Fear ye not, stand still, and see the salvation of the LORD, which he will shew to you to day: for the Egyptians whom ye have seen to day, ye shall see them again no more for ever.*

Salvation is attaining God's righteousness. We are never called to seek righteousness by our own moral attempts to obey the law. We are instructed to seek God's righteousness, which is salvation.

Matthew 6:33 — *But seek ye first the kingdom of God, and his righteousness; and all these things shall be added unto you.*

Notice that it says to seek His righteousness. It doesn't say to try to be righteous on your own or seek your own righteousness. That would be meaningless. (Philippians 3:9.)

Salvation is God's. But we can make it ours through faith in Jesus.

Genesis 49:18 — *I have waited for thy salvation, O Lord.*

1 Chronicles 16:23 — *Sing unto the LORD, all the earth; shew forth from day to day his salvation.*

Some people may object to this by saying that this is not referring to eternal salvation but temporal salvation. I hardly think that anyone who would praise God for salvation would be praising Him for temporal salvation when we are still in a world of disasters and peril. The only salvation that is praiseworthy is eternal salvation.

Salvation is of the Lord but He wants to give it to us. We need to overemphasize this point. God doesn't need to be saved, saying that salvation is of the Lord simply means that He does all the work in saving us.

1 Chronicles 16:35 — *And say ye, Save us, O God of our salvation, and gather us together, and deliver us from the heathen, that we may give thanks to thy holy name, and glory in thy praise.*

Psalm 20:5 — *We will rejoice in thy salvation, and in the name of our God we will set up our banners: the LORD fulfil all thy petitions.*

Psalm 27:1 — *The LORD is my light and my salvation; whom shall I fear? the LORD is the strength of my life; of whom shall I be afraid?*

Salvation is of the Lord, but it is offered to us to be our salvation. The reason for this chapter is to let all believers know that they don't play any role in saving themselves. We must stop this horrid epidemic called: Lordship salvation. We must stop taking credit in our salvation. This of the Lord and something He freely gives us.

Psalm 35:9 — *And my soul shall be joyful in the LORD: it shall rejoice in his salvation.*

Faith needs no work.

~ 8 ~

Perfect

What must I do to go to heaven? You must be perfect! Matthew 5:48 says: *Be ye therefore <u>perfect</u>, even as your Father which is in heaven is perfect.*

The Bible confirms this reality. YOU MUST BE PERFECT! Period.

That's it. Case closed. Nobody's going to heaven. We can all go home, order a pizza and play dominos all night.

Honestly, are we perfect?

Romans 3:23 — *For all have sinned, and come short of the glory of God.*

See. The Bible says that we all have sinned. We are all sinners. So nobody is perfect.

So, what makes us perfect?

Our own works. Sacraments. Following the law. Turning from sin.

No.

Hebrews 7:19 — *For the law made <u>nothing</u> perfect, but the bringing in of a better hope did; by the which we draw nigh unto God.*

This better hope is a presage of Christ's arrival. Only He can make us perfect because He is perfect.

Hebrews 10:14 — *For by one offering he hath <u>perfected</u> for ever them that are sanctified.*

This "one" offering is referring to Christ's sacrificial death for our sins.

Once is enough!

Romans 6:10 — *For in that he died, he died unto sin <u>once</u>: but in that he liveth, he liveth unto God.*

Christ perfected us.

Colossians 1:28 — *Whom we preach, warning every man, and teaching every man in all wisdom; that we may present every man <u>perfect</u> in Christ Jesus.*

His perfection becomes ours' through transference once we put faith in him. Our sins are also fully paid for.

Jeremiah 33:8 — *And I will cleanse them from <u>all their iniquity</u>, whereby they have sinned against me; and I will pardon <u>all their iniquities</u>, whereby they have sinned, and whereby they have transgressed against me.*

This verse provides double assurance that all our sins are paid for in Christ.

So if you want to be perfect and go to heaven all you have to do is acknowledge you're a sinner and put faith in Christ.

Psalm 32:5 — *I acknowledge my sin unto thee, and mine iniquity have I not hid. I said, I will confess my transgressions unto the LORD; and thou forgavest the iniquity of my sin. Selah.*

Christ will make you perfect in the sight of God despite the fact that you continue to fall short everyday.

John 17:23 — *I in them, and thou in me, that they may be made <u>perfect</u> in one; and that the world may know that thou hast sent me, and hast loved them, as thou hast loved me.*

This is the bottom line. We either accept Christ's righteousness as our title to perfection or we trust our own righteousness. Martin Luther maintained that this is the doctrine by which the church stands or falls. Justification by faith alone. If this doctrine falls, then we've got major problems considering that nobody knows how works can save them.

We do know how Christ saves us. Through his blood, death, burial and resurrection. (Colossians 1:14) If this doctrine falls, then this book falls with it and so does the entire gospel message of the Bible. Some people think that if we believe in faith alone, we are putting ourselves in a dangerous risk!

I think that by trusting in anything additional to faith alone we are putting ourselves in unforeseeable peril. If it's not by faith alone then it must be by works.

Matthew 7:22 — *Many will say to me in that day, Lord, Lord, have we not prophesied in thy name? and in thy name have cast out devils? And in thy name done many wonderful <u>works</u>?*

Keyword, "works."

Now read on.

Matthew 7:23 — *And then will I profess unto them, <u>I never knew</u> you: depart from me, ye that <u>work</u> iniquity.*

That brings us back to faith.

But what about man's righteousness?

Take a look at.

Ezekiel 33:13 — *When I shall say to the righteous, that he shall surely live; if he <u>trust</u> to his <u>own</u> <u>righteousness</u>, and commit iniquity, all his righteousnesses shall not be remembered; but for his iniquity that he hath committed, he shall die for it.*

This is not talking about losing salvation when it says, "die for it". This is talking about a person trusting in his own righteousness much like the Pharisees, Sadducees and modern day legalists. This verse is proof that when a man trusts in his own righteousness, he will still commit iniquity.

Obviously, he is still carnal and carnality vitiates our nature. If a man trusts in his own righteousness it is a foregone conclusion that he will still be in sin. Therefore, sin erases the idea of having this man's righteousness remembered or commemorated, and he shall physically die because of his iniquities. This is proof alone that we need to put on Christ's righteousness in order to be perfect.

Job 29:14 — *I put on righteousness, and it clothed me: my judgment was as a robe and a diadem.*

Notice it doesn't say that I can be righteous on my own comparable to Christ's holy, blameless righteousness. Instead, it illustrates a person putting on righteousness akin to putting on a shirt.

How do we do this?

Faith alone in Christ alone!

Free Not Cheap!

~ 9 ~

Galatianism

Question: What is Galatianism? Answer: It is the idea that man is saved by grace but that works maintain his salvation. The epistolary preface to Galatians states: The Galatians having launched their Christian experience by faith, seem content to leave their voyage of faith and chart a new course based on works—a course Paul finds disturbing.

In essence, Paul was contending for the true gospel that had been perverted by the church of Galatia. Most people in some way or another have added works into their soteriology or theology. Even I, myself have questioned other's salvation because I saw nary a good work coming from them. I have to remember that my criterion for good works has been increasingly hyperspiritualized. But still, this is demanding some kind of lawful deed to transpire from people that say that they are Christians.

The problem with Galatianism is that it makes the demand for salvation by law a counterfeit substitute for faith.

Paul was strident in his words:

Galatians 3:1 — *O foolish Galatians, who hath bewitched you, that ye should not obey the truth, before whose eyes Jesus Christ hath been evidently set forth, crucified among you?*

Free grace theology has much scriptural evidence in the book of Galatians.

Galatians 6:18 — *Brethren, the grace of our Lord Jesus Christ be with your spirit. Amen.*

Grace is not grace unless it is by faith alone.

Romans 4:16 — *Therefore it is of faith, that it might be by grace; to the end the promise might be sure to all the seed; not to that only which is of the law, but to that also which is of the faith of Abraham; who is the father of us all.*

Read the first sentence of this verse again and memorize it.

Therefore it is <u>of faith</u> that it might be <u>of grace.</u>

In other words, it couldn't be pure grace unless it was by pure faith.

Galatians backs this up.

Galatians 3:22 — *But the scripture hath concluded all under sin, that the promise by faith of Jesus Christ might be given to them that believe.*

Galatians 3:11 — *But that no man is justified by the law in the sight of God, it is evident: for, The just shall live by faith.*

Galatians 3:14 — *That the blessing of Abraham might come on the Gentiles through Jesus Christ; that we might receive the promise of the Spirit through faith.*

Galatians 3:17 — *And this I say, that the covenant, that was confirmed before of God in Christ, the law, which was four hundred and thirty years after, cannot disannul, that it should make the promise of none effect.*

Reverting back to a system of law destroys this promise. Anyone that denies free grace has made the Abrahamic promise of none effect. This is a much more serious matter then most realize.

Galatianism is flinging man into a tortuous labyrinth of impossibility. For the law is impossible to completely obey.

Galatians 6:13 — *For <u>neither they themselves who are circumcised keep the law</u>; but desire to have you circumcised, that they may glory in your flesh.*

Even the Galatianists (law-keepers) aren't keeping the law. What hypocrites!

The law curses and likewise puts people under a curse.

Galatians 3:10 — *For as many as are of the works of the law are under the curse: for it is written, Cursed is every one that continueth not in all things which are written in the book of the law to do them.*

Christ has removed this curse; Galatianism puts man back under it.

Galatians 3:13 — *Christ hath redeemed us from the curse of the law, being made a curse for us: for it is written, Cursed is every one that hangeth on a tree.*

Galatianism denies true grace and nullifies Christ's finished work on the cross.

Galatians 5:4 — *Christ is become of no effect unto you, whosoever of you are justified by the law; ye are fallen from grace.*

Fallen from grace doesn't mean losing salvation as some confused people may suggest. This simply means falling from an understanding of grace, which can only be done by trying to be justified by the law, which was the purpose for Paul writing this epistle. Galatianism had doctrinally corrupted the church of Galatia and such corruption is still extant in the church today.

The reason I preach or write on free grace is because it is biblically consistent. I've been persecuted for writing books on theology and this is to be expected. If I were not being led by God to write this then such persecution would have been condign, but since the gospel is under siege in most churches, the need for the free grace message must be defended and delivered.

Paul defended it and so shall I.

It's a tragedy when Galatianism infiltrates into a church. It doesn't take much. All you have to do is add one infinitesimal work to grace and grace is fully soiled and no more grace. (Romans 11:6.) A little leaven leaveneth the whole lump. (Galatians 5:9.)

All it takes is one suggestion that grace and works flow together and you've imposed Galatianism. I've heard someone say that grace is like one leg and works were like the other, without one you would precariously topple to the ground. This is a subtle form of adding works to grace. My theory is that grace is like both legs and you stand in it without works.

Good works may be what the legs are producing out of gratitude, but in no wise do they bolster the footing!

Galatians 2:21 — *I do not frustrate the grace of God: for if righteousness come by the law, then Christ is dead in vain.*

Free Not Cheap!

~ 10 ~

Getting the Gospel Right

This chapter explains what the Gospel IS. Faith in Jesus. Trust in Him alone as the object of your salvation.

1 John 5:1 — *Whosoever believeth that Jesus is the Christ is born of God: and every one that loveth him that begat loveth him also that is begotten of him.*

John 6:47 — *Verily, verily, I say unto you, He that believeth on me hath everlasting life.*

These two verses along with hundreds of others explain to us how to receive the gospel, but what is the gospel?

1 Corinthians 15:3–4 — *For I delivered unto you first of all that which I also received, how that Christ died for our sins according to the scriptures; And that he was buried, and that he rose again the third day according to the scriptures.*

This is the account of the gospel straight from scripture. John 3:16, 18, 36, 5:24, 6:47, and other such Sola Fide verses tell us how to receive the gospel. Believe in the Lord Jesus Christ.

Here is a good order to present and explain the gospel.

Revelation 22:17.

Romans 6:23.

Romans 3:23–24.

1 Corinthians 15:3–4.

John 3:16.

John 6:47.

Acts 16:29–31.

What the Gospel Is Not

Good works.

Scripture is clear that works, no matter how good, could never earn us salvation.

Titus 3:5 — *Not by works of righteousness which we have done, but according to his mercy he saved us, by the washing of regeneration, and renewing of the Holy Ghost.*

Romans 4:5 — *But to him that worketh not, but believeth on him that justifieth the ungodly, his faith is counted for righteousness.*

Faith plus works.

Romans 4:16 — *Therefore it is of faith, that it might be by grace; to the end the promise might be sure to all the seed; not to that only which is of the law, but to that also which is of the faith of Abraham; who is the father of us all.*

Romans 11:6 — *And if by grace, then is it no more of works: otherwise grace is no more grace. But if it be of works, then it is no more grace: otherwise work is no more work.*

Salvation is either by grace through faith or it doesn't exist. Grace and works don't mix.

Faith plus works in order to prove that you are saved.

2 Corinthians 13:5 — *Examine yourselves, whether ye be in the faith; prove your own selves. Know ye not your own selves, how that Jesus Christ is in you, except ye be reprobates?*

This examination is not about salvation. It is about discipleship. Paul was worried that his own faith would get shipwrecked. No amount of examination would ever suffice in knowing that someone is saved without requiring some form of evidential works. We can examine whether or not we are in fellowship with God. Am I reading my Bible, praying, or am I cussing and telling dirty jokes. This type of examination is necessary in deciphering whether or not we are in active fellowship with God.

Faith plus repentance or turning from sins.

Turning from sins is a work.

Jonah 3:10 — *And God saw their works, that they turned from their evil way; and God repented of the evil, that he had said that he would do unto them, and he did it not.*

It doesn't say that God saw their works, and they turned from their evil ways. This is not two sequential actions. The comma describes this as one act. God saw their works (comma) and these works are described as turning from evil ways.

Clearly, repentance in this sense is a work.

Repentance is not bearing fruit and is supplanted by bearing fruit.

Matthew 3:8 — *Bring forth therefore fruits meet for repentance.*

"Meet" in the Greek is Axios, which literally means compared to or in lieu of repentance. It should read as: "Bring forth therefore fruits in lieu of repentance." This totally excludes this type of repentance. What this should say is that we should stop trying to turn from our sins and instead just bear fruit. Anyone can (think they) stop sinning and meanwhile do nothing good. See also Luke 3:8.

Think about this logically.

I can't stop lusting.

I can't stop lusting.

Wallowing around in this kind of useless attempt to stop sinning is a total waste of time. You're not going to ever stop lusting so get off your duff and go soul winning. This is the difference between "stop sinning" and "bearing fruit."

Faith plus being willing to turn from sins.

Being willing to turn from sins is work, especially if your sin is a harrowing addiction. We don't have to do anything to accept a physical gift and we don't have to be willing to do anything contrary to accepting the gift. So no, you don't have to be willing to turn from sin in order to be saved.

Romans 9:16 — *So then it is not of him that willeth, nor of him that runneth, but of God that sheweth mercy.*

Young's literal translation.

So, then – not of him who is willing, nor of him who is running, but of God who is doing kindness.

The only thing that we have to be willing to do is accept the free gift of salvation. Being willing to turn from sins is a tradeoff. God is not saying: "I'll give you salvation if you are willing to turn from sin." Nope. Salvation is a GIFT!

Faith plus deep contrition or agony over sins.

We don't have to be sorry for our sins before we get saved. We must be cognizant that we are sinners but the expression of contrition or sorrow should come after you are saved.

Philippians 2:12 — *Wherefore, my beloved, as ye have always obeyed, not as in my presence only, but now much more in my absence, work out your own salvation with fear and trembling.*

This verse does not teach salvation by works. Work out your salvation, not work for your salvation. Once we are saved we should shed tears over our sins and over the fact that Christ suffered for our sins by his sacrificial death.

Faith that endures. (Perseverance of the saints.)

Romans 3:3–4 — *For what if some did not believe? shall their unbelief make the faith of God without effect? God forbid: yea, let God be true, but every man a liar; as it is written, That thou mightest be justified in thy sayings, and mightest overcome when thou art judged.*

Clearly, this is not persevering, as Calvinists like to assert as being part of salvation. God remains faithful even when we fail to be.

See also, 1 Corinthians 1:9.

Faith plus baptism.

Acts 16:29–31 — *Then he called for a light, and sprang in, and came trembling, and fell down before Paul and Silas, And brought them out, and said, Sirs, what must I do to be saved? And they said, Believe on the Lord Jesus Christ, and thou shalt be saved, and thy house.*

Paul and Silas said nothing about water baptism. If it were necessary then why did they leave it out of their gospel message? Obviously, literal water baptism has no role in salvation whatsoever. It is the initial act of obedience and is simply symbolic of the death, burial and resurrection of Christ.

Faith plus verbal confession.

Romans 10:10 — *For with the heart man believeth unto righteousness; and with the mouth confession is made unto salvation.*

Salvation here is through the heart not the mouth. Imputed righteousness is synonymous to salvation. Confession is simply a command that confirms that we are saved.

Faith plus obeying the law or the Ten Commandments.

Galatians 2:16 — *Knowing that a man is not justified by the works of the law, but by the faith of Jesus Christ, even we have believed in Jesus Christ, that we might be justified by the faith of Christ, and not by the works of the law: for by the works of the law shall no flesh be justified.*

Works, obeying the law, or any other ritualistic activity is excluded by the faith alone message of the gospel.

Romans 10:4 — *For Christ is the end of the law for righteousness to every one that believeth.*

The end of the law means that there is now no law. Do we have to obey the law to se saved? What law? The law unto righteousness came to an end by Christ through our faith in him.

The gospel is simple. It can be spoken in 25 words.

John 3:16 — *For God so loved the world, that he gave his only begotten Son, that whosoever believeth in him should not perish, but have everlasting life.*

I entitled this Getting The Gospel Right. I hope that we will stick with the book of John and its purpose and get the gospel right. (John 20:30–31.)

Faith needs no work.

~ 11 ~

<u>Know</u> You Are Going to Heaven

Many Christians when asked if they are saved will respond with "yes," but when asked if they are going to heaven will give a different response. They may say something like. "I don't know" or "I hope so" or I'm about 90 percent sure. The damnable doctrine of Lordship Salvation makes knowing if you are going to heaven an uncertainty.

Some Lordship Salvationists will say that they are 99 percent sure that they are going to heaven. Scripture refutes this nonsense. If you are a proponent of Lordship Salvation you have zero percent certainty that you are going to heaven—ZERO! Your trust is either partly on self or entirely on self.

Trust in Christ gives us certainty.

Lordship Salvationists will subtlety say that if you aren't obeying Christ or living right then you aren't trusting Christ. Wrong! This is not trusting Christ at all. Obedience is trusting in self. Imagine being rescued by a fireman but then the fireman says to you, you aren't holding onto me tight enough, so you really aren't trusting in me. I better let you go back into the fire. It makes no difference how tight we hold onto Christ or how much we obey Him; he holds on to us and He was obedient enough to satisfy God's anger when He went to the cross. (John 10:28–29.)

The bottom line is this. Nobody could have certainty that they are going to heaven if our human merit is interjected into the equation of salvation.

But the Bible wants us to be sure.

Here's a verse that makes salvation a certainty.

Proverbs 29:25 — *The fear of man bringeth a snare: but whoso putteth his trust in the LORD shall be safe.*

Assurance of salvation is what God wants all believers to have.

It doesn't get any clearer than John's first epistle. His audience knew they were saved. It is absurd to suggest that his audience wasn't exclusively believers.

All Lordship Salvation does is produce self-righteous neo-Pharisees. It's a systemic machine that manufactures arrogant snobs. It also gives no one any real assurance that they're going to heaven. Am I good enough says the Doubting Thomas? Yes, I AM good enough says the Lordship Salvationist—unless he's having a bad day.

Whether you're a Lordship Salvationist or not, so many people think that their main goal in life is to get to heaven. Such people just don't get it. If your goal is to get to heaven you are trying to work for your salvation. Such an attempt is selfish. You should know that as a believer you are undoubtedly going to heaven. Your goal in life, after being fully aware of this should be to get others into heaven, soul-winning, being Christlike, bearing fruit, pleasing God, earning heavenly rewards. This whole "I hope I make it to heaven" or "making it to heaven is all that matters" is selfish non-sense when God promises it to all believers.

It would be like my friend giving me 100 dollars and then me, after procuring it, wondering if I really possessed it—crisping it between my forefinger and thumb, feeling the realness of its texture but yet still wondering if it is real. This is paranoia, doubt, skepticism, and unbelief. Christians don't have to ask or beg to be saved. They must realize that God offers salvation freely. (John 4:10.) All they have to do is take it by believing in Christ for it!

Let's not make our goal getting to heaven. That was God's goal in sending his only begotten son to the cross to die for our sins. Let's make our focus on heaven.

First of all, we establish that heaven is real. The first verse in the Bible declares that it is.

Genesis 1:1 — *In the beginning God created the heaven and the earth.*

Galatians 3:26 — *For ye are all the children of God by faith in Christ Jesus.*

Children of God are promised heaven.

Romans 6:5 — *For if we have been planted together in the likeness of his death, we shall be also in the likeness of his resurrection.*

Psalm 89:29 — *His seed also will I make to endure for ever, and his throne as the days of heaven.*

Faith needs no work.

Being confident of this very thing, that he which hath begun a good work in you will perform it until the day of Jesus Christ.— Philippians 1:6.

~ 12 ~

Eternal Security
(Perseverance of the Saviour)

2 Thessalonians 3:5. NIV — *May the Lord direct your hearts into God's love and Christ's perseverance.*

I've read many books and online articles on eternal security. Some good, ... some not so good. Although all the ones I've read seemed to be supportive of this doctrine very few seemed to represent it correctly and biblically. For some good books on eternal security, read: Eternal Security, Can You Be Sure? By Charles Stanley or read: Once Saved always Saved, by Lloyd A Olson.

Sad to say, some of the material I've read about eternal security was destitute of biblical truth and self-contradictory. Here is an excerpt from a faulty article on eternal security.

"The bottom line is, we are safe in Christ as long as we continue to live in Jesus (Hebrews 10:19–23). We have full assurance of faith in him, because it is he who saves us. We don't have to worry, 'Am I going to make it?' In Christ we have assurance—we are his and are saved, and nothing can snatch us out of his hand."

Take a look at:

"As long as WE continue to live in Jesus."

This is not eternal security. It is conditional security. Man is not guaranteed to follow Christ and furthermore nobody knows if they are currently following Christ well enough. This article is as Arminian in nature as an anti-eternal security article. Because it puts the security back on man and his ability to follow Christ, which is indefinable, anyway you look at it.

Psalm 118:8 — *It is better to trust in the LORD than to put confidence in man.*

I'm not putting my confidence in myself or any other man when it comes to eternal security. It's either all in Christ or non-existent. Also see: Jeremiah 9:23–24.

Our confidence needs to be in God.

Ephesians 3:11–12 — *According to the eternal purpose which he purposed in Christ Jesus our Lord: In whom we have boldness and access with confidence by the faith of him.*

To believe that we have security as long as we follow Christ is to put that security in ourselves, which is no security at all. The Bible clearly instructs us not to put confidence in the flesh.

Philippians 3:3 — *For we are the circumcision, which worship God in the spirit, and rejoice in Christ Jesus, and have no confidence in the flesh.*

Matthew 26:41 — *Watch and pray, that ye enter not into temptation: the spirit indeed is willing, but the flesh is weak.*

We were born sinners (Psalm 51:5. Romans 3:23.)

We are easily deceived.

Deuteronomy 11:16 — *Take heed to yourselves, that your heart be not deceived, and ye turn aside, and serve other gods, and worship them.*

We are weak.

Psalm 6:2 — *Have mercy upon me, O LORD; for I am weak: O LORD, heal me; for my bones are vexed.*

We are constantly tempted.

Galatians 6:1 — *Brethren, if a man be overtaken in a fault, ye which are spiritual, restore such an one in the spirit of meekness; considering thyself, lest thou also be tempted.*

Weak, fickle, fleshly, oft-tempted and sinful. That is what we are. Is there really any hope in trusting in ourselves for security? NOPE!

We need God to secure us. And He does.

Psalm 18:32 — *It is God that girdeth me with strength, and maketh my way perfect.*

Eternal security is true and needs to be correctly represented. Some may say that the words "eternal security" aren't in the Bible. But this is a strawman argument for the words: "rapture," "trinity," "theology," or even "Bible" aren't in the Bible." But just because the words are not found in the Bible doesn't mean that the concept doesn't exist? You could stanch this argument only if the arguer is willing to relent on his position. But if someone is hell-bent on going to hell, which is what they all should be because that would be the inevasible outcome to all who want to lose their salvation, then there is no hope in enlightening them.

But if a person is open-minded and reasonable, then proving eternal security shouldn't be that difficult.

The words "eternal security" are not found in the Bible in sequence, but they are found in the Bible. The KJV is accurate and even clear in certain verses. For instance, John 5:24 is a three-point hitter in backing up eternal security.

But for the sake of the "it's-not-in-the-Bible" argument, look at:

Hebrews 9:12. NLT — *Once for all time he took blood into that most holy place, but not the blood of goats and calves. He took his own blood, and with it <u>secured</u> our salvation forever.*

It doesn't get any clearer than in this verse.

If someone still wants to argue or disagree, then be done with them and allow prayers and God's discipline to awaken them.

All the scripture, proof-texts, divine revelation and reasoning in the world isn't going to change someone's mind who doesn't want to give up their false doctrine. Some have accused me of being just as adamant, and some have even said that my belief was just my opinion. Well, it's also the Bible's opinion. One should be adamant and dogmatic when it comes to the truth. The apostle Paul was.

Galatians 1:6–7 — *I marvel that ye are so soon removed from him that called you into the grace of Christ unto another gospel. Which is not another; but there be some that trouble you, and would pervert the gospel of Christ.*

Denying eternal security is perverting the gospel.

Here are some verses on eternal security.

Salvation is from God. He saves, justifies and grants sinners eternal life.

Exodus 14:13 — *And Moses said unto the people, Fear ye not, stand still, and see the <u>salvation of the LORD</u>, which he will shew to you to day: for the Egyptians whom ye have seen to day, ye shall see them again no more for ever.*

Also see, Jonah 2:9 and Psalm 3:8.

Once you are saved, nothing can undo it. Nothing!

Ecclesiastes 3:14 — *I know that, whatsoever God doeth, it shall be for ever: nothing can be put to it, nor any thing taken from it: and God doeth it, that men should fear before him.*

Salvation is eternal. Security is eternal. This is so easy to grasp, yet scores of Christians deny it.

John 17:3 — *And this is life eternal, that they might know thee the only true God, and Jesus Christ, whom thou hast sent.*

Paul believed in eternal security prior to accepting the gospel.

Romans 4:20–22 — *He staggered not at the promise of God through unbelief; but was strong in faith, giving glory to God; And being fully persuaded that, what he had promised, he was able also to perform. And therefore it was imputed to him for righteousness.*

Notice that Paul was persuaded of eternal security and then his faith was imputed to him for righteousness.

We are preserved in Christ. This is eternal security.

Jude 1:1 — *Jude, the servant of Jesus Christ, and brother of James, to them that are sanctified by God the Father, and <u>preserved</u> in Jesus Christ, and called.*

Eternal security is scripturally consistent and scripture plentifully supports it.

Here is a huge list of OSAS scriptures.

John 3:16. John 5:24. John 6:47. John 10:28–29. John 6:37. John 11:25–26. John 17:6–9. John 14:16. Romans 8:1. Romans 5:10. Romans 8:28–29. Romans 8:38–39. Romans 11:29. Ephesians 1:6. Ephesians 4:30. Philippians 1:6. Hebrews 5:13. Hebrews 12:2. Hebrews 10:14. Hebrews 7:25. 1 Peter 1:4–5. 1 Thessalonians 5:23. 2 Timothy 1:9. 2 Timothy 2:11–13. Jude 1:24.

Jeremiah 32:40. Psalm 37:28. Psalm 89:29–34. Psalm 125:2. Isaiah 32:17. Isaiah 42:6. Isaiah 45:16–17. Isaiah 49:8. Isaiah 49:14–17. Nehemiah 9:17.

I subtitled this chapter "Perseverance Of The Saviour." The common Calvinistic doctrine: Perseverance of the Saints or even the preservation of the saints is too self-oriented and works based. This is real, biblical eternal security.

John 4:14 — *But whosoever drinketh of the water that I shall give him shall never thirst; (ONCE SAVED) but the water that I shall give him shall be in him a well of water springing up into everlasting life. (ALWAYS SAVED.)*

Eternal Security is the gospel.

Calling eternal security a side issue is no different than calling the gospel a side issue. Imagine a bunch of missionaries saying to each other.

"Should we preach the gospel?"

"I don't know. It's just a side issue."

Well that is what we do when we put the doctrine of eternal security on the proverbial table, thus labeling it a: "side issue." Some may disagree and say that you can still preach the gospel without embracing the doctrine of eternal security. True, but that is a false gospel. One in which gives partial glory to Christ and partial glory to man. Partial glory to an infinite, all-sufficient Saviour is totally shunning Christ and insulting Him in the process.

If you don't support the doctrine of eternal security, you are calling God a liar and disbelieving the gospel. Saying that I don't believe in eternal security or that eternal security is a damnable heresy is tantamount to saying I don't believe the gospel and that the gospel is damnable heresy!

This is why I personally try to avoid those who deny eternal security or O.S.A.S.

Now, this book is not about eternal security thematically speaking, but eternal security is like one branch of the tree of free grace theology, so it is important that I devote more material on it.

Salvation is given to us from above.

John 3:3 — *Jesus answered and said unto him, Verily, verily, I say unto thee, Except a man be born again, he cannot see the kingdom of God.*

John 3:7 — *Marvel not that I said unto thee, Ye must be born again.*

"Born again" in Greek is gennatha anothen, which literally means born from above. This new birth is from God. It is fool-hardy to think that it is something that can be revoked by something mortal man can do. Eternal security is founded by the fact that salvation is something God does. It is of God, not us.

Acts 28:28 — *Be it known therefore unto you, that the <u>salvation of God</u> is sent unto the Gentiles, and that they will hear it.*

Losing salvation could only be possible if man could save himself. Scripture is clear that God saves us for it is God that justifies us as well.

Romans 8:33 — *Who shall lay any thing to the charge of God's elect? It is God that justifieth.*

Salvation is established before the world began.

2 Timothy 1:9 — *Who hath saved us, and called us with an holy calling, not according to our works, but according to his own purpose and grace, which was given us in Christ Jesus before the world began.*

Titus 1:2 — *In hope of eternal life, which God, that cannot lie, promised before the world began.*

There is no way to undo salvation. Eternal life was promised to us, (the saved) before the world existed. The only way to undo it, which the deniers of eternal security believe that you can do, would be to time travel back to when the world didn't exist and then do whatever it takes to be lost again—then and there! If we had the power to do that, which is absurd, then <u>yes</u> you could lose your salvation. Not only is this absurd but this would quash God's plan for us.

Not embracing eternal security denies justification, forensic imputation, adoption and predestination. It also denies the finished work of Christ. If something was declared true before the world began, you can rest assure that nothing can cancel it during this worldly lifetime. Because that declarative cancellation would have to also be documented before time, space and the world began. The record would have to go something like this. The elect who non-fatalistically chose Christ were saved and given eternal life. This was established before the world began according to Titus 1:2 but because the elect decided he didn't want to be saved anymore during this lifetime, eternal life was likewise cancelled and the cancellation was established before the world began. This is nonsense and the Bible says nothing about such drivel. Losing salvation is more childish and ridiculous than a grown man sucking his thumb! No offence.

Salvation is given to us now.

Salvation in Greek is soteria in the plural sense and soterion in the singular sense, which is a neuter of the adjectival sense. Plural, meaning both eternal and temporal salvation. This usage of salvation is referring to eternal salvation.

Philippians 1:18–20 — *What then? notwithstanding, every way, whether in pretence, or in truth, Christ is preached; and I therein do rejoice, yea, and will rejoice. For I know that this shall turn to my salvation through your prayer, and the supply of the Spirit of Jesus Christ, According to my earnest expectation and my hope, that in nothing I shall be ashamed, but that with all boldness, as always, so now also Christ shall be magnified in my body, whether it be by life, or by death.*

Other usages may be speaking explicitly of temporal deliverance.

Hebrews 11:7 — *By faith Noah, being warned of God of things not seen as yet, moved with fear, prepared an ark to the <u>saving of his house</u>; by the which he condemned the world, and became heir of the righteousness which is by faith.*

But in some cases it is referring to both eternal and temporal.

Romans 13:11 — *And that, knowing the time, that now it is high time to awake out of sleep: for now is our salvation nearer than when we believed.*

Now is our salvation. In the eternal sense it is describing salvation as being a present possession. The previous portion of this chapter describes salvation as a past possession. "Before the world began." But this verse describes salvation as a present possession, not something that may or may not come posthumously. Salvation, in full, has been given to us now; if it could be lost or forfeited it wouldn't be true salvation unless you could find a way to antonymize the words salvation and everlasting life. You can't.

Deniers of eternal security are simply saying that John 3:16 and John 6:47 are not true.

Revelation 12:10 — *And I heard a loud voice saying in heaven, <u>Now is come salvation</u>, and strength, and the kingdom of our God, and the power of his Christ: for the accuser of our brethren is cast down, which accused them before our God day and night.*

Some might say that this is a prophetic verse suggesting that it is referring to when salvation really takes place. Well, maybe, but if I'm reading this verse now and have trusted in Christ by faith alone then I have salvation now.

2 Corinthians 6:2 — *For he saith, I have heard thee in a time accepted, and in the day of salvation have I succoured thee: behold, now is the accepted time; behold, now is the day of salvation.*

Salvation is sealed.

2 Corinthians 1:21–22 — *Now he which stablisheth us with you in Christ, and hath anointed us, is God; Who hath also sealed us, and given the earnest of the Spirit in our hearts.*

Denying eternal security always causes one to misinterpret scripture. Always! I've read an article that said that this seal could be broken if a Christian kept on sinning. What kind of a seal would that be?

Greek for "sealed": Sphragizo, means "to seal" and is used to indicate security and permanency. How on earth can it be broken? How on earth can something permanent become impermanent? If something can become impermanent how in the world was it ever really permanent? The only way around this precious truth is to lie, molest, wrangle, redefine, twist and contort the context of scripture and that is what all deniers of eternal security are doing! Period.

Ephesians 4:30 — *And grieve not the holy Spirit of God, whereby ye are sealed unto the day of redemption.*

SEALED UNTO THE DAY OF REDEMPTION! Not sealed until it could somehow be broken which is erroneous heresy. This verse says that the seal is until the day of redemption. In no wise does it say that the seal can be broken or annulled. It is only liars that say this! Your salvation is permanently sealed the very nanosecond you believe in Christ for salvation. Eternal security is the very crux of the gospel. Calling it a side issue after knowing this is a putrid malediction!

Salvation means that all sins are covered.

All sins are forgiven.

Mark 3:28 — *Verily I say unto you, All sins shall be forgiven unto the sons of men, and blasphemies wherewith soever they shall blaspheme.*

Colossians 2:13 — *And you, being dead in your sins and the uncircumcision of your flesh, hath he quickened together with him, having forgiven you all trespasses.*

Leviticus 16:30 — *For on that day shall the priest make an atonement for you, to cleanse you, that ye may be clean from all your sins before the LORD.*

This was symbolic for what Christ was going to do upon his arrival. The sacrifice made by the high priest and then later by Christ Himself covered all man's sins. Past, present and future. Imagine losing your salvation by sinning. You would have to discard the preceding verses. That's dishonest as is any attempt to refute eternal security. Now imagine supporting the all-sins-covered doctrine but suggesting that salvation can be volitionally forfeited. You get mad at God and say the heck with this salvation. I want nothing more to do with it. You go on angry and sin carelessly. Your sins are still covered and you are still declared righteous in the sight of God. How could salvation be lost?

The only thing that keeps a person from heaven is sin and spiritual deadness. Once you are saved, you've taken care of the spiritual deadness part.

Romans 6:11 — *Likewise reckon ye also yourselves to be dead indeed unto sin, but alive unto God through Jesus Christ our Lord.*

Christ took care of the sin part; your initial faith took care of the spiritual deadness through forensic justification. What on earth can keep a saved person from heaven? The answer is nothing. A friend of mine said that why would God allow someone to enter heaven if they refused it? Well. God's promise is a promise. If He denied heaven to any one of His once saved always saved children, he would be a promise-breaker.

Hebrews 13:5 — *Let your conversation be without covetousness; and be content with such things as ye have: for he hath said, I will never leave thee, nor forsake thee.*

God can't forsake His children. We may forsake God as many of us do from time to time. The question is whether or not we are being chastised. I don't believe that a true child of God would blithely say forget this salvation junk and then happily go on with his life as if being a TV-junky was more exciting than being a saved Christian. That doesn't make sense and reeks of false conversion. But for a true child of God to forsake God is a recipe for ongoing misery!

The fact is that if we really place faith in Christ for salvation, we are eternal secure. NO MATTER WHAT!

Assurance of salvation is clearly stated in scripture.

Some may say that there is a difference between assurance of salvation and eternal security and there is. Eternal security is objective—an objective reality. Assurance of salvation is subjective. If a person lives in sin he may lose his assurance. No amount of sin can cause a person to lose his eternal security, but Satan through lies and deception is deft in causing our personal, subjective assurance to falter. The differential is simply subjective versus objective. But the reality is that the Bible does have the words "assurance of salvation" in it. The question is whether or not you are going to believe it.

Hebrews 6:11 — *And we desire that every one of you do shew the same diligence to the full assurance of hope unto the end.*

In my King James Bible right before 1 John 5 and verse 6 it says as a headline: Assurance of salvation.

John 11:25 — *Jesus said unto her, I am the resurrection, and the life: he that believeth in me, though he were dead (will physically die), yet shall he live. (Eternally, spiritually.) And whosoever liveth (physically) and believeth (get saved) in me shall never die. (Spiritually, which is eternal security) Believest thou this?*

Jesus tells her that she has eternal security and then He goes on further by telling her to believe it!

1 John 5:13 — *These things have I written unto you that believe on the name of the Son of God; that ye may <u>know</u> that ye have eternal life, and that ye may believe on the name of the Son of God.*

So many people say that this is simply talking about what we must do to know that we are saved. Deniers of eternal security have to add indefinite acts of works, but the scripture plainly states that this knowledge is simply due to belief in Christ. Written unto you that believe in Christ that you may know that you have eternal life. That's assurance of salvation. That's eternal security.

Closing statements on "eternal security is the gospel."

God promises eternal life. If it could be lost or forfeited in anyway it wouldn't be eternal. It would have to bear another title but scripture doesn't flounder in meaning when it describes salvation. Denying eternal security once again just flat-out contradicts simple biblical logic and truth. As stated before, here's the verse that gives triple homage to eternal security — a three-point proof-text.

John 5:24 — *Verily, verily, I say unto you, He that heareth my word, and believeth on him that sent me, hath everlasting life, and shall not come into condemnation; but is passed from death unto life.*

"Hath everlasting life" ... equals eternal security! "Shall not come into condemnation" ... equals eternal security! "Is passed from death unto life" ... equals eternal security! It doesn't get any clearer. This doctrine is irrefutable whilst under proper hermeneutical scrutiny and is not only essential to the gospel but is the gospel. If you're not eternally secure; you are not saved. All saved people who honestly put faith in Christ are eternally secure whether they realize it or not.

God's word is settled.

Psalm 119:89 — *For ever, O LORD, thy word is settled in heaven.*

Nehemiah 9:17 — *And refused to obey, neither were mindful of thy wonders that thou didst among them; but hardened their necks, and in their rebellion appointed a captain to return to their bondage: but thou art a God ready to pardon, gracious and merciful, slow to anger, and of great kindness, and <u>forsookest them not</u>.*

Once Saved Always Saved.

~ 13 ~

Can a Christian Live Any Way He Wants... And Still Go to Heaven?

YES! People ask that question often and many Christians don't have an answer for them. But to the asker that may object to my seemingly crazy answer, you need to recognize that you live anyway you want to and are expecting to go to heaven when you die—all the same. Some may object and say that a person who calls himself a Christian but goes on living any way they want to won't go to heaven. But the objector needs to realize that he lives any way he wants to as well. Any objection to this assertion is simply a byproduct of pride.

Hypothetically speaking, for the guy who goes out drinking and sleeping around yes he is living in sin. But so is the other guy who decides to take a break from his Bible reading to watch two hours of television whilst enjoying a root beer float. Isn't he selfishly doing what he wants to do as well?

So let me re-ask the question.

Can a Christian live any way he wants and still go to heaven?

I'm going to give you the same answer:

YES!

Yes. Yes. Yes!

But this is the wrong question.

The asker should've asked.

Can a Christian live any way he wants and be in a right fellowship with God?

Can a Christian live any way he wants and go without physical consequences?

Can a Christian live any way he wants and not lose rewards in heaven?

Can a Christian live any way he wants and avoid a guilt complex?

Can a Christian live any way he wants and have a valid witness or testimony?

Can a Christian live any way he wants without contrition or chastisement?

Can a Christian live any way he wants without doubting his salvation.

Can a Christian live any way he wants without persecution?

Can a Christian live any way he wants and not see how foolish he is being?

Can a Christian live any way he wants without eventually getting burnout?

Can a Christian live any way he wants and still have all his prayers answered?

Can a Christian live any way he wants and be happy?

The answer to all of these questions is: NO!

Saved yes, in good stead with God, no.

We are called to live after the spirit. Galatians 5:25. The Bible also makes it clear that sin is only enjoyable for a season. Hebrews 11:25.

Every single Christian I've ever met that objected to the fact that a Christian couldn't live any way they wanted to and still go to heaven was hypocritically living any way they wanted to! Even living a holy life is self-willed. But aside from that all Christians even at their best are sinners. (Psalm 39:5.) It's sickening to think that such ignorance about sin pervades Christendom.

I've even heard some famous preachers and evangelists say that, yes a Christian can live any way they want to and still go to heaven but if you are a true Christian, you won't want to live in sin any longer. Wrong! What does the Bible say about this? Take King Solomon for instance; let's see if he didn't enjoy his sin.

1 Kings 11:1 — *But king Solomon loved many strange women, together with the daughter of Pharaoh, women of the Moabites, Ammonites, Edomites, Zidonians, and Hittites.*

Honestly, is a married man allowed to love women other than his spouse? Wouldn't such love really be idolatrous lust? Wouldn't this anti-monogamy be a grave sin? Yeah, and it said that Solomon loved these womenic idols. Where does one go off in saying that Christians don't desire to sin any longer? Read on.

1 Kings 11:4 — *For it came to pass, when Solomon was old, that his wives turned away his heart after other gods: and his heart was not perfect with the LORD his God, as was the heart of David his father.*

Solomon was saved. How do I know?

1 Kings 3:3 — *And Solomon loved the LORD, walking in the statutes of David his father: only he sacrificed and burnt incense in high places.*

But according to the scriptures in chapter 11, he was living any way he wanted to. Any Christian that objects to the idea that true Christians won't live any way they want to fail to understand that they themselves live any way they want to.

Am I condoning sin? No, I hate it. Well actually my spirit hates it but my flesh loves it. That's why I put such a great emphasis on spiritual living in my preaching and Bible teachings. But the Bible is clear that even carnal, living-any-way-they-want-to Christians will in fact go to heaven.

1 Thessalonians 5:9–10 — *For God hath not appointed us to wrath, but to obtain salvation by our Lord Jesus Christ, Who died for us, that, whether we wake or sleep, we should live together with him.*

'Sleep' is not a reference to "physical naptime sleep" or being physically dead, (which is Koimao) but it is a reference to carnality. How do I know this, take a look at?

1 Thessalonians 5:5–6 — *Ye are all the children of light, and the children of the day: we are not of the night, nor of darkness. Therefore let us not sleep, as do others; but let us watch and be sober.*

Why would Paul say, "let us not sleep?" Did he mean physical naptime sleep? Was he pro-insomnia? No, and furthermore, why would he say, "let us not sleep" if he meant, "let us not be physically dead." Let us not sleep means let us not be carnal or unspiritual. That's why he exhorted them to be sober and watchful. He wanted them to avoid spiritual torpescence.

This type of "spiritual torpor" sleep in the Greek is Katheudo, (1 Thessalonians 5:10, Ephesians 5:14 and Mark 13:36.) The concordance says in verbatim, that Katheudo means: of carnal indifference to spiritual things on the part of the believer. And a condition of insensibility to divine things involving conformity to the world.

There you have it ... carnal Christians.

Mark 13:35–36 — *Watch ye therefore: for ye know not when the master of the house cometh, at even, or at midnight, or at the cockcrowing, or in the morning: Lest coming suddenly he find you sleeping (Living carnal.)*

Ephesians 5:14 — *Wherefore he saith, Awake thou that sleepest (living carnal), and arise from the dead, and Christ shall give thee light.*

So yes, there you have true born again Christians that are living carnal or anyway they want to live that are on their way to heaven. I don't like carnal living for I'm guilty of it everyday and so is everyone else, (Ecclesiastes 7:20, Romans 3:23. 1 John 1:8, 10). But despite the fact that I don't like it that there are Christians that aren't living for God AT ALL, I can't let my biases, prejudices, proclivities and personal opinions stand in direct opposition of what the Bible clearly teaches.

Secure In Christ.

And Jesus said unto them, Because of your unbelief: for verily I say unto you, If ye have faith as a grain of mustard seed, ye shall say unto this mountain, Remove hence to yonder place; and it shall remove; and nothing shall be impossible unto you. — Matthew 17:20.

~ 14 ~

Faith or Faithfulness

2 Thessalonians 3:3 — *But the Lord is faithful, who shall stablish you, and keep you from evil.*

A weighty question in theology is whether or not we are saved by faith or saved by ongoing faithfulness. Covenant theologians and Works Salvationists have changed the simple means of biblical faith into faithfulness and they do so disingenuously only to foist upon others their heretical doctrine. Sure, faithfulness is commendable but to make it a demand for salvation is heresy. Ephesians 2:8 states that we are saved by faith—a one time act of faith. This faith is in the aorist tense meaning one act of faith that continues on forevermore.

The real question is whose faith gets us to heaven. God's or ours'. Where man has faith and some men are faithful, it is ALWAYS God's faithfulness that gets us to heaven even when we lose faith or fall short in some other manner. The word 'faith' only appears twice in the Old Testament. Deuteronomy 32:20 and Habakkuk 2:4. In Deuteronomy, the faith mentioned is man's faith. The Hebrew word here is, Enum.

Deuteronomy 32:20 — *And he said, I will hide my face from them, I will see what their end shall be: for they are a very froward generation, children in whom is no faith.*

This describes man's faith and in this instance a child's faith, which was far from faithful. Faithful or faithfulness is always

Emanuh, which literally means firmness or security. God is always faithful when it comes to salvation.

Here is a list of scriptures that describe man's faith and God's faithfulness.

Nehemiah 7:2.   Hebrew: Emeth. Man's faith.

1 Samuel 26:23. Hebrew: Emanuh. God's faithfulness.

Numbers 12:7.   Hebrew: Aman. Man's faith.

Deuteronomy 32:20. Hebrew: Emun. Man's faith.

Psalm 5:9. Hebrew: Kun. Man's faith.

Psalm 12:1. Hebrew: Aman. Man's faith.

Psalm 36:5. Hebrew: Emanuh. God's faithfulness.

Psalm 31:23. Hebrew: Aman. Man's faith.

Psalm 40:10. Hebrew: Emanuh. God's faithfulness.

Psalm 101:6. Hebrew: Aman. Man's faith.

Psalm 88:11. Hebrew: Emanuh. God's faithfulness.

Psalm 89:5. Hebrew: Emanuh. God's faithfulness.

Proverbs 11:13. Hebrew: Aman. Man's faith.

Proverbs 20:6. Hebrew: Emun. Man's faith.

Isaiah 8:2. Hebrew: Aman. Man's faith.

Isaiah 25:1. Hebrew: Emanuh. God's faithfulness.

Habakkuk 2:4. Hebrew: Emanuh. God's faithfulness.

Emanuh always refers to faithfulness, whether it is God's faithfulness or man's. But God's faithfulness is what guarantees us salvation. Take a look at:

1 Samuel 26:23 — *The LORD render to every man his right-eousness and his faithfulness; for the LORD delivered thee into my hand to day, but I would not stretch forth mine hand against the LORD's anointed.*

To reiterate, faithfulness in Hebrew is Emanuh. It characterizes firm, full, solid faith—unlike man's faith. But the words 'faithful' or 'faithfulness' don't always have to be used in order to be of the same Hebrew: Emanuh. Look at:

Habakkuk 2:4 — *Behold, his soul which is lifted up is not upright in him: but the just shall live by <u>his faith</u>.*

The just or "saved" shall live by God's faith. Or in layman's terms: we have salvation because God is faithful. The "his faith" is synonymous to faithfulness only because God's faith in terms of salvation is always <u>faithful</u>! The word 'faith' in this verse is Emanuh only because it is characterizing God's faithfulness in keeping believers saved no matter what they do or do not do.

Even in the New Testament is God's faithfulness described.

1 Corinthians 1:9 — *God is faithful, by whom ye were called unto the fellowship of his Son Jesus Christ our Lord.*

There is not a clearer verse in the Bible that proves that it is God's faithfulness that keeps us saved.

The Greek for faith in this case is Pistis. In the account of lacking faith or minimal faith as in Matthew 6:30 where Jesus says: 'O ye of little faith' the Greek word for faith is Oligopistos, which literally means, "small faith." But the Greek for <u>faithful</u> as found in 1 Corinthians 1:9 is, Pistos, which means trustworthy, sure and true. This is God's faith. The faith that is ours as found in Ephesians 2:8 is simply to be persuaded or convinced that what God says is true is in fact true. Man is never goaded to be faithful in order to be saved, he is commanded to just have faith in Christ for salvation. God is faithful!

God's faithfulness settles our salvation. (Psalm 119:89.)

Some people may be thinking that yeah I guess Christians can lose a little faith from time to time and God remains faithful, but what about if a Christian loses <u>all his faith</u> and forsakes God?

Take a look at:

Romans 3:3 — *For what if some did not believe? shall their unbelief make the faith of God without effect?*

The Greek for 'unbelief' in this verse is Apistia, which means faithlessness. This is the only Greek word for faithlessness appertaining to believers. This is not the same Greek tense as in Apisteo or in Apietheia, which pertains only to lost people. (See Mark 9:19, 1 Timothy 5:8.) Apisteo can literally mean, "without Christ". Apistia is referring to when a Christian loses his faith in God. Romans 3:3, is referring to when a Christian has lost his faith completely. St. Paul asks the question rhetorically.

Shall their unbelief make the faith of God without effect?

Verse 4 answers in two words.

God forbid!

This is pure proof that even if we lose our faith in God; His faithfulness keeps us saved. This is good news and knowing this should paradoxically make us want to strengthen our faith in God. Hebrews 13:5, says that God will never leave us or forsake us. This is His promise even to those who unfortunately forsake Him.

In conclusion.

1 Corinthians 10:13 — *There hath no temptation taken you but such as is common to man: but <u>God is faithful</u>, who will not suffer you to be tempted above that ye are able; but will with the temptation also make a way to escape, that ye may be able to bear it.*

God is faithful in every capacity. For salvation, help in need, comfort, security, the works. We should never think that our faithfulness to the end is what is saving us. Because if someone asks us if we are saved, you'd have to say I don't know yet for the end of my faith hasn't come.

1 Thessalonians 5:24 — *Faithful is he that calleth you, (God) who also will do it.*

SECURE IN CHRIST!

As for me, I will call upon God; and the LORD shall save me. — Psalm 55:16.

~ 15 ~

OT Free Grace

So many Christians are confused about the Old Testament. They will tell you that we are under grace but the Old Testament church was under the law. Grace superceded the law after the crucifixion. This is not true and it is the other way around. The church was always under grace. For the church to be under the law in the Old Testament and then later during the new testamentary dispensation under grace would make God a mind-changer and even dispensationally unfair. Scripture declares:

Hebrews 13:8 — *Jesus Christ the same yesterday, and to day, and for ever.*

When I said that grace superceding the law was the other way around, I simply meant that grace came first and then came the law, but only to reveal transgressions and the impossibility of being saved by the law.

Acts 13:39 — *And by him all that believe are justified from all things, from which ye could not be justified by the law of Moses.*

The Old Testament was under grace as well as we are.

The law was given 430 years after God made the covenantal promise with Abraham. The law was given for two reasons. One, to show Israel the seriousness of sin. And two because they didn't want to be under grace and preferred to be under the law. Evidently, they had this do-it-yourself complex as the opponents of free grace do today.

Exodus 19:8 — *And all the people answered together, and said, All that the LORD hath spoken we will do. And Moses returned the words of the people unto the LORD.*

This was Israel asserting that they had, within their own humanoid power, the ability to obey the law. If they knew how impossible the law was to keep in its entirety, they wouldn't have been so presumptuous as to say: all that the Lord hath spoken we will do.

To the contrary, as helpless sinners, we might say something like this.

"I'm saved by grace!"

But this was not the attitude of Israel nor is it the attitude of anyone that denies free grace. God knew that the only way Israel or anyone for that matter, could be saved was by grace. But Israel insisted on saving themselves by their own works so God had no choice but to establish them the horrendously unkeepable law they opted for.

Exodus 19:9–12 — *And the LORD said unto Moses, Lo, I come unto thee in a thick cloud, that the people may hear when I speak with thee, and believe thee for ever. And Moses told the words of the people unto the LORD. And the LORD said unto Moses, Go unto the people, and sanctify them to day and to morrow, and let them wash their clothes, And be ready against the third day: for the third day the LORD will come down in the sight of all the people upon mount Sinai. And thou shalt set bounds unto the people round about, saying, Take heed to yourselves, that ye go not up into the mount, or touch the border of it: whosoever toucheth the mount shall be surely put to death.*

Scripture describes God's change of mind toward Israel as dismal.

Exodus 19:16 — *And it came to pass on the third day in the morning, that there were thunders and lightnings, and a thick cloud upon the mount, and the voice of the trumpet exceeding loud; so that all the people that was in the camp trembled.*

Had Israel stuck with free grace and not desired to be under the burdensome law, God would have not given them a reason to tremble. Even modern-day anti-free-gracers tremble from time to time and if they don't they SHOULD, because scripture clearly states that anyone who doesn't obey the entire law is cursed. (Galatians 3:10.)

It was the law they wanted and the law they got and the penalties thereof were just as austere as the harshness of the law. This does not mean that grace was removed and thereby supplanted by the law. This simply means that grace had unto it added the law. The message of the law as clearly stated is: whosoever toucheth the mount shall be surely put to death.

This is to show Israel the stridency and hopelessness of the law. The message of free grace is antithetical to this.

The law screams in your face, *do this, do that, thou shalt, thou shalt not!*

Grace tells us of what our wonderful Saviour has done for us.

Romans 5:8 — *But God commendeth his love toward us, in that, while we were yet sinners, Christ died for us.*

From the beginning, the law message was this:

Genesis 2:17 — *But of the tree of the knowledge of good and evil, thou shalt not eat of it: for in the day that thou eatest thereof thou shalt surely die.*

This tells you what to do and then of the horrible consequences of what will happen if you don't obey.

Grace, however, tells you how easy it is to be saved.

Mark 11:30 — *For my yoke is easy, and my burden is light.*

When you add the law to this simple understanding of grace you have a heavy and difficult yoke to bear. Jesus refutes this. Salvation is always by grace. Old Testament, New Testament, intertestamentary times as well. The Bible is clear that grace must be the sole condition for salvation.

Acts 15:11 — *But we believe that through the grace of the LORD Jesus Christ we shall be saved, even as they.*

Free Not Cheap!

~ 16 ~

Calvinism Refuted
The tulip has been plucked!

Calvinism's tulip is heresy. Calvinism is a system of theology that seems to soteriologically outline or delineate the salvation process. However, it is highly inclined towards double predestinearianism or partial redemptionism, which posit that some people go to heaven beyond their volition and others go to hell beyond their volition. Nothing could be farther from the truth. No one is predestined or appointed to hell without having a chance to choose Christ.

1 Thessalonians 5:9 — *For God hath not appointed us to wrath, but to obtain salvation by our Lord Jesus Christ.*

Let's break down every point of T.U.L.I.P. and let the Bible refute each point.

Total depravity. (Or inability.)

Unconditional election.

Limited atonement.

Irresistible grace.

Perseverance of the saints.

TOTAL DEPRAVITY (INABILITY)

The idea is that man has no ability to accept Christ through faith so God has to predetermine who will be saved. The rest of the world is damned beyond their control. God does arbitrarily save the elect according to this doctrine. If you are one of the elect, you will be given irresistible grace—which is also a gift. In other words, if you are one of His elect, you will automatically come to God only because you were fatalistically elected. The Calvinist will use these verses to backup this doctrine.

Romans 3:11 — *There is none that understandeth, there is none that seeketh after God.*

All this simply means is that nobody can come to God or seek Him without God drawing them.

John 6:44 — *No man can come to me, except the Father which hath sent me draw him: and I will raise him up at the last day.*

God wants everyone to come to Him, (John 3:16) but we must make a choice to stop resisting Him. It is true that people, after divine illumination, can and do seek God.

Proverbs 28:5 — *Evil men understand not judgment: but they that seek the LORD understand all things.*

Man is totally depraved and sinful as Romans 3:23 states, but man is not totally unable to come to Christ. The "T" in tulip is bogus.

According to scripture we do have free will.

Revelation 22:17 — *And the Spirit and the bride say, Come. And let him that heareth say, Come. And let him that is athirst come. And whosoever <u>will</u>, let him take the water of life freely.*

Unconditional Election

This is the idea that election is unconditional and that it's not up to us exercising free will.

Scripture gives us a choice.

John 3:18 — *He that believeth on him is not condemned: but he that believeth not is condemned already, because he hath not believed in the name of the only begotten Son of God.*

DL Moody said that you have two types of people. Those who say, "I will" to Christ and those who say "I won't." There is no I can't because I'm not elect. This scripture clearly refutes unconditional election.

John 5:40 — *And ye will not come to me, that ye might have life.*

Notice it says you <u>will</u> not come to me. It doesn't say you <u>cannot</u> come to me. Calvinism is heresy!

LIMITED ATONEMENT

This is the idea that Christ only died for the elect. The atonement of the cross is limited only to the predetermined elect. If you're not the elect then atonement wasn't made for you, they say. Scripture clearly asserts that Christ died for everyone not just the elect. However the sacrifice for sins has no effect on those that reject it.

1 John 2:2 — *And he is the propitiation for our sins: and not for ours only, but also for the sins of the whole world.*

Hebrews 4:2 — *For unto us was the gospel preached, as well as unto them: but the word preached did not profit them, not being mixed with faith in them that heard it.*

The reason the gospel did not profit them was because they refused to accept salvation by faith. But they could have and it would have profited them as it did those who came to faith in Christ.

2 Peter 2:1 — *But there were false prophets also among the people, even as there shall be false teachers among you, who*

privily shall bring in damnable heresies, even denying the <u>Lord</u> <u>that bought them</u>, and bring upon themselves swift destruction.

God bought the salvation for the lost, false teachers but they refused to accept it. It doesn't get any clearer that Christ died for everyone.

Christ died...

1. For all (1 Timothy 2:6; Isaiah 53:6).

2. For every man (Hebrew. 2:9).

3. For the world (John 3:16).

4. For the sins of the whole world (1 John 2:2).

5. For the ungodly (Romans. 5:6).

6. For false teachers (2 Peter 2:1).

7. For many (Matthew 20:28).

8. For Israel (John 11:50–51).

9. For the Church (Ephesians. 5:25).

10. For "me" (Galatians. 2:20).

IRRESISTIBLE GRACE

This is the idea that we can't accept grace freely but that it's irresistible. If you are one of the elect, according to this doctrine, then God's grace is totally irresistible and nobody elected has the ability to resist it. What does scripture say about this? Calvinists try to claim that everyone God draws to him will come to Him. (John 6:44.). They claim that 'draw' in the Greek, helkuo helko, means to drag, which in some cases it does but in this verse it means to prepare or prim.

John 12:32 — *And I, if I be lifted up from the earth, <u>will draw</u> <u>all men</u> unto me.*

If Calvinism is correct and if this means that God drags us without resistance then universalism is also correct and that all will be saved according to this verse.

The Bible is clear that God does want all men to be saved but we can resist the Holy Spirit.

Romans 13:2 — *Whosoever therefore resisteth the power, resisteth the ordinance of God: and they that resist shall receive to themselves damnation.*

Looks like the Bible doesn't support this irresistible grace nonsense.

PERSEVERANCE OF THE SAINTS

This is the idea that all true born-again Christians will persevere in the faith to prove that they are saved. If one falls away or doesn't persevere they prove to have not been truly saved. This is nonsense and leaves no assurance of salvation until after a person is dead.

Luke 8:13 — *They on the rock are they, which, when they hear, receive the word with joy; and these have no root, which for a while believe, and in time of temptation fall away.*

They received salvation with joy, believed for a while and then fell away due to temptation. Another problem with P.O.T.S. is that it places too high an emphasis on man persevering instead of God keeping His children kept by His power.

1 Peter 1:5 — *Who are kept by the power of God through faith unto salvation ready to be revealed in the last time.*

It is God who keeps us by His power. One act of faith on our part activates God's keeping power. I've heard people say that this promise was contingent upon our faith but that would comparatively undermine God's marvelous keeping power. Some people use this verse as a proof-text for P.O.T.S., but the correct scriptural context is being neglected.

Take a look at this verse.

Matthew 24:13 — *But he that shall endure unto the end, the same shall be saved.*

This is talking about enduring tribulation and being saved physically and temporally. This is not talking about being saved unto eternal life for John makes the only condition for salvation in his gospel: faith or belief, never endurance, which would connote works or continued faithfulness. The word saved here in Greek is Sozo, which is a reference to temporal or physical salvation. Compare this to:

Matthew 8:25 — *And his disciples came to him, and awoke him, saying, Lord, save us: we perish.*

The word save is the same Sozo, which according to the concordance is exclusively used to denote temporal deliverance. Scripture clearly and easily refutes all five points of Calvinism's tulip. There will be more on this in the chapter entitled: Arminianism Refuted.

Secure In Christ.

~ 17 ~

Assurance of Salvation

Those who deny eternal security need to not read this for it will benefit you nil! The truth is not in you until you can embrace the doctrine of biblical assurance based solely on scripture. I've had it up to here with people giving others subjective means of assurance for salvation. I'll give you a few subjective ways of having assurance of salvation. They're good but nevertheless insufficient.

Good works.

Spiritual growth. You must have been born again if you are growing spiritually.

Overcoming certain sins.

New mindset, new attitude.

Others affirm that you are saved.

Prayers.

Love for God and others.

The devil's got me doubting, only saved people doubt whether they have been saved or not.

These are all great but they are also labile and not always fail-safe.

For instance...

Good works may not measure up to some manmade standard. We quench the spirit on a daily basis. Our new attitude or mindset could get bogged down with negativism. Our prayers may seem vain. Our love for God and others may fluctuate depending on how they treat us.

Subjective assurance just doesn't always cut it. To think that someone can have assurance of salvation based on how they live makes God's word not as reliable!

Objective assurance however is failsafe. It is only found in God's word. God wants us to know that we are his elect. (1 Thessalonians 1:4.)

Arminians don't believe in permanent, irreversible election and common Calvinists tend to make a Christian uncertain if they are truly one of the elect based on reference to lifestyle or whatnot. This is all unbiblical! Take a look at some verses that prove that God does want us to have full assurance of salvation.

1 Thessalonians 1:4–5 — *Knowing, brethren beloved, your election of God. For our gospel came not unto you in word only, but also in power, and in the Holy Ghost, and in much assurance; as ye know what manner of men we were among you for your sake.*

Titus 3:4–7 — *But after that the kindness and love of God our Saviour toward man appeared, Not by works of righteousness which we have done, but according to his mercy he saved us, by the washing of regeneration, and renewing of the Holy Ghost; Which he shed on us abundantly through Jesus Christ our Saviour; That being justified by his grace, we should be made heirs according to the hope of eternal life.*

Verse 7 gives us assurance of salvation.

Read this from the NLT.

Because of his grace he declared us righteous and gave us <u>confidence</u> that we will inherit eternal life.

It sounds like God wants us to be totally confident that we have eternal life.

1 John 5:13 — *These things have I written unto you that believe on the name of the Son of God; that ye may <u>know</u> that ye have eternal life, and that ye may believe on the name of the Son of God.*

God wants us to know that we are saved. In the same Johannine epistle this point is reiterated.

1 John 5:19–20 — *And we <u>know</u> that we are of God, and the whole world lieth in wickedness. And we know that the Son of God is come, and hath given us an understanding, that we may know him that is true, and we are in him that is true, even in his Son Jesus Christ. This is the true God, and eternal life.*

AND WE KNOW THAT WE ARE OF GOD!

Sounds like they had assurance of salvation and solely based on the word of God.

In the letter to Romans Paul wanted the all believers to know that they had salvation.

Romans 4:16 — *Therefore it is of faith, that it might be by grace; to the end the <u>promise might be sure</u> to all the seed; not to that only which is of the law, but to that also which is of the faith of Abraham; who is the father of us all.*

ONLY SAVED PEOPLE DOUBT, EXPLAINED

Think about it. You get a new motorcycle. You leave it in your backyard either unprotected or minimally protected. You worry about it getting rained on, stolen or tainted in some other way. Logically, you have such sentiments and ideations toward the motorcycle because it's yours and it exists. Imagine someone else not worrying about his motorcycle at all. He doesn't worry because he doesn't have one to worry about. Same with salvation. Salvation is a gift, a real gift that God gives to all who believe in him. John 3:16.

Some people don't worry about whether or not they have lost their salvation, which is impossible, or whether or not they still have their salvation because they have never been saved. They have no salvation to think about whether in a negative or positive light.

I'm not saying that all those people who don't doubt their salvation weren't ever saved, but as CH Surgeon put it, those who have never doubted their salvation are probably not saved. I partially disagree with his statement for some people are just too optimistic to doubt their salvation.

But is it good to doubt your salvation?

I think at first it is, because it gets newbie Christians thinking and digging into the scripture. It proves that Satan is our enemy and that he causes doubt. But after growing up in the faith, a constant doubt of salvation is simply expressing distrust to God's word and is a sin.

John 6:47 — *Verily, verily, I say unto you, He that believeth on me hath everlasting life.*

If you believe in Jesus for salvation now or at any time in the past, this verse confirms that you are doubtlessly saved. To squelch such doubt when Satan tries to deceive you, one needs to repeat this verse until Satan flees. One needs also to remind Satan where he is going. To the lake of fire. (Revelation 20:10.)

In fact, read this verse to Satan and then laugh at him!

But what about those people that try to make you think that your faith wasn't true, "saving faith." Well they are heretics! There's only one kind of faith when it comes to salvation. Faith is being convinced that something is true. Jesus says that in order to be saved we need to believe on Him.

You either know that you've believed on Him or not. My friend put it nicely. If salvation is simply believing in Jesus then I'm saved; if it's anything else ... then I'm not. According to the Bible it is not by anything else other than faith. Those who try to dichotomize or qualify faith are liars plain and simple. Faith is putting trust in Christ and not in your own works.

Assurance of salvation is simple.

1 Thessalonians 2:2 — *But even after that we had suffered before, and were shamefully entreated, as ye know, at Philippi, we were bold in our God to speak unto you the gospel of God with much contention.*

Boldness and assurance go hand-in-hand.

Q: Why do people doubt their salvation?

A: Because they feel like they don't do enough for God. They fail to realize that Christ did it all. He did enough! Christ's death pleased God.

Isaiah 53:10 — *Yet it pleased the LORD to bruise him; he hath put him to grief: when thou shalt make his soul an offering for sin, he shall see his seed, he shall prolong his days, and the pleasure of the LORD shall prosper in his hand.*

Assurance of salvation is essential. Those who deny this doctrine are placing assurance in themselves and not on the full sufficiency of Christ.

Secure In Christ.

Wherefore he is able also to save them to the uttermost that come unto God by him, seeing he ever liveth to make intercession for them. — Hebrews 7:25.

~ 18 ~

Arminianism Refuted!
Examining Hebrews 6:4–6.
Rewards versus salvation.

I hope you enjoyed the chapter where I refuted Calvinism. I would never use Arminianism to refute Calvinism nor would I use Calvinism to refute Arminianism. I did and will use the free grace position to refute both heretical systems.

The common Arminian view is this. If you don't persist in the faith, then you will lose salvation. Some extremists will say that you can lose your salvation if you sin—every time you sin. This just makes the Arminian heresy laughably heretical.

Arminians use verses like this to suggest that persistent faith is what saves.

Matthew 10:22 — *And ye shall be hated of all men for my name's sake: but he that endureth to the end shall be saved.*

See, there it is, you gotta endure to the end. (They say)

Well is this salvation meant to be eternal salvation?

Tom Constable comments.

"But he that shall endure unto the end, the same shall be saved. The disciples would find themselves opposed by everyone without distinction including their own family members, not just rulers. In spite of such widespread and malicious persecution the disciple must endure patiently to the end. "The end" refers to the end of this period of intense persecution, namely, the Tribulation.

The second coming of the Son of Man will end it (v. 23). The promise of salvation for the one who remains faithful does not imply eternal salvation since that depends on faith in Jesus. It is deliverance from the period of intense persecution that is in view. Entrance into the kingdom would constitute salvation for these future persecuted disciples."

Arminians use other verses to support their heresy such as: Matthew 24:13, Mark 13:13. Hebrews 6:15.

But lets look at one that I have heard two people use to back up their "faithfulness to the end" doctrine:

Revelation 2:10 — *Fear none of those things which thou shalt suffer: behold, the devil shall cast some of you into prison, that ye may be tried; and ye shall have tribulation ten days: be thou faithful unto death, and I will give thee a crown of life.*

The crown of life is not synonymous to eternal life as the people I know are maintaining. Each crown has a significant meaning. All are in the sense of rewards, whereas salvation is a fee gift (Romans 6:23, 5:15–18, John 4:10, Ephesians 2:8–9, Isaiah 61:1.)

Here are the crowns that will be given as rewards.

Incorruptible crown
It is earned by leading a disciplined life.

1 Corinthians 9:25 — *And every man that striveth for the mastery is temperate in all things. Now they do it to obtain a corruptible crown; but we an incorruptible.*

Crown of rejoicing
It is earned by discipleship and evangelism.

1 Thessalonians 2:19 — *For what is our hope, or joy, or crown of rejoicing? Are not even ye in the presence of our Lord Jesus Christ at his coming?*

Crown of Glory

It is earned by shepherding God's flock.

1 Peter 5:4 — *And when the chief Shepherd shall appear, ye shall receive a crown of glory that fadeth not away.*

Crown of righteousness

It is earned by loving the Lord's appearing.

2 Timothy 4:8 — *Henceforth there is laid up for me a crown of righteousness, which the Lord, the righteous judge, shall give me at that day: and not to me only, but unto all them also that love his appearing.*

A carnal Christian who is spiritually asleep will not be receiving this crown. For he clings to the things of this world and is not anticipating the rapture or the second coming of Christ. (Parusia.)

Crown of life

It is earned by enduring trials.

James 1:12 — *Blessed is the man that endureth temptation: for when he is tried, he shall receive the crown of life, which the Lord hath promised to them that love him.*

Those who struggle in this life will receive this crown. It is not the same as eternal life. One must never confuse the gift of salvation with rewards. The reference in Revelation 2:10 is not as clear as the reference in James for in James says blessed is the man. "Blessings" always pertain to rewards.

It is obvious that enduring to the end has nothing to do with salvation as Arminianism wrongly postulates. Another portion of scripture that Arminians us is Hebrews 6:4–6.

Hebrews 6:4–6 — *For it is impossible for those who were once enlightened, and have tasted of the heavenly gift, and were made partakers of the Holy Ghost, And have tasted the good word of God, and the powers of the world to come, If they shall fall away, to renew them again unto repentance; seeing they crucify to themselves the Son of God afresh, and put him to an open shame.*

In my view this is referring to true believers. Verses 4 and five make it clear that this is referring to Christians.

So what does this mean when it says? "If they shall fall away."

Take a look at:

Hebrews 3:12 — *Take heed, brethren, lest there be in any of you an evil heart of unbelief, in departing from the living God.*

Those who fall away, for them it is impossible to renew then unto repentance.

Hebrews 3:13 — *But exhort one another daily, while it is called To day; lest any of you be hardened through the deceitfulness of sin.*

Sin deadens the conscience. The more we commit sins the easier it is to rationalize it. This is an exhortation not to harden your hearts. The are four traditional views.

VIEW #1: LOSS OF SALVATION.

Real Christians have fallen away and lost salvation.

According to this view they can't ever be resaved for they have rejected the only means to be saved.

I call this "Too late" theology or one-chance soteriology. This is absurd. Get saved, five minutes later fall away. You have salvation for five minutes and now you are eternal doomed! This is the deadliest heresy imaginable!

VIEW #2: HYPOTHETICAL LOSS OF SALVATION.

The second view believes the same as the first Arminian view. Real Christians, loss of salvation, can't get it back. The only difference is that this view deems this to be hypothetical. They focus on the word "if" and suggest that if you could fall away and lose salvation, you could never get it back so therefore this proves that it can't be lost. It is simply a hypothetical warning to discourage people from falling away.

Not a bad view for it still fortifies the doctrine of security. I used to hold to this view. The only problem is that the suggestion of this being a hypothesis is also a hypothesis.

VIEW #3: LOSS OF SERVICE.

The third view posits the loss of service. If we stop believing in Christ whether we go back to Judaism or even agnosticism, we will not be useful anymore. This view is not speaking about those who temporarily lost faith in Christ due to adventitious influence, worldly pleasure, doubt, or persecution, in such cases it is not so problematic to repent and follow Christ anew. This is talking about those hard cases where people deliberately reject Christ after truly being saved. This is similar to the hardening of Pharaoh's heart. When a person becomes so staunch in their unbelief, their heart is hardened and that is why it is impossible for them to repent. Hebrews 6 is a warning for the Messianic Jews not to revert back to full Christless Judaism. (This I feel is the correct view.)

VIEW #4: FALSE CHRISTIANS FALL AWAY

The forth view posits that these tasters of the heavenly gifts were just tasters and not swallowers. They had superficial engagements with Christian things but did not appropriate them for salvation. This view holds that these fallen Jews were never saved.

So which view is correct?

I believe the Bible supports the third view. Here's why.

Take a look at verse 8.

Hebrews 6:8 — *But that which beareth thorns and briers is rejected, and is nigh unto cursing; whose end is to be burned.*

This is talking about losing rewards. The reference to burning is not talking about eternal damnation or hellfire. But of burning one's works. Those who fall away are not bearing fruit but are bearing thorns and briers. Thorn and briers denote works being burned up. See 1 Corinthians 3:11–15.

Hebrews 6:9 — *But, beloved, we are persuaded better things of you, and things that accompany salvation, though we thus speak.*

The writer of Hebrews expects better things of these Christians. In other words, he expects them not to fall away—although alas some may. He's given them this warning so that they won't apostatize, but it doesn't guarantee that they will heed this warning. This is an encouragement to be faithful and bear fruit, not a threat to damn the faithless that are bearing thorns and briers.

Hebrews 6 is simply an instruction manual for keeping the faith and being diligent. Read verse 1.

Hebrews 6:1 — *Therefore leaving the principles of the doctrine of Christ, let us go on unto perfection; not laying again the foundation of repentance from dead works, and of faith toward God.*

Now read verse 11.

Hebrews 6:11 — *And we desire that every one of you do shew the same diligence to the full assurance of hope unto the end.*

Conclusion, v 6:4–6 clearly has nothing to do with salvation. Because the only threat to those who fall away is having one's rewards burned up! Verse 8. Verse 11 is about assurance of salvation. Those who fall away don't have this assurance howbeit they still have salvation.

Eternal security is clearly taught in the Bible: (John 5:24. Psalms 89:29, Romans 8:38–39, John 10:27–29, John 11:25. Ephesians 4:30, Hebrews 7:25, John 3:16. Jeremiah 32:40.)

Arminianism is false!

Calvinism is false!

You have three common views.

View #1: If you don't persevere you lose salvation.

View #2: If you don't persevere you prove you never had salvation.

View #3: If one falls away he will return in order to prove that he was truly saved. If he doesn't come back it proves he isn't saved. The problem with one and two is that they are essentially saying the same thing and are both conjectural because scripture doesn't back them up. The problem with number three is that nobody knows whether or not the fallen Christian will return! (Essentially, view three is saying the same as two; it's just more optimistic.)

The fourth view—which is not traditional—is what I feel is the correct view.

View #4: You can't lose salvation or (give it back.)

If you do fall away, you are still saved whether or not you return to the faith! But if you are truly saved, God will deal with you. How He deals (chastens) with you is up to Him and in no wise determined by man's speculation.

This view adheres to scriptural logic and is the safest view.

Hebrews 13:5, says it all. *Let your conversation be without covetousness; and be content with such things as ye have: for he hath said, I will never leave thee, nor forsake thee.*

Secure In Christ!

And why call ye me, Lord, Lord, and do not the things which I say? — Luke 6:46.

~ 19 ~

Lordship Salvation Is Heresy

If I had the monetary and incendiary wherewithal to do so, I'd buy every book that promotes Lordship Salvation and burn them to ash!

So many people who embrace Lordship salvation whether they know it or not have changed the gospel. Lordship salvation is works salvation anyway you look at it. I wrote an article about works salvation that I have not included in this book because of its overt causticity. I will interpolate an excerpt here and there.

There are saved people out there that are afraid that God will send them to hell if they don't live right. These people know nothing of God's grace, His love or His fatherhood. I would never claim that God is love but then say that He might send me to hell if I don't live a certain way. Who can lay anything to charge of God's elect for it is God that justifieth. Pretty clear!

I plan to integrate bits and pieces of this article throughout this chapter.

Lordship salvation demands holy living. It demands repentance. It demands that people forsake their sins. It makes the gospel different for everyone. Faith alone is not the gospel according to Lordship salvation. For instance, if one person has a bad habit like smoking cigarettes, then according to Lordship salvation, he must have faith in Christ and give up smoking. Now for someone who is addicted to porn, cigarettes, alcohol, illegal drugs, gossip, overeating, television, shopping, etc ... the gospel for him becomes tenfold, taxing, and impossible.

If Lordship salvation were true then everyone would be given a different gospel. It gives those who have lived a life in the ghetto and have undergone a lifestyle of utter depravity no hope! Demanding that someone must forsake his or her sins is ludicrous. The gospel never changes and has been the same for everyone since the beginning of time.

Jesus doesn't change.

Hebrews 13:8 — *Jesus Christ the same yesterday, and to day, and for ever.*

See also, Malachi 3:6.

If Lordship salvation were true then NO ONE could be saved! Furthermore NO ONE could know in this lifetime that they were saved which is unbiblical. (1 John 5:13.)

Nobody is obedient enough! Nobody has completely made Christ the Lord of his or her life. And nobody even knows what it means to make Christ the Lord of their life. Lordship Salvation is baseless nonsense! Christ is Lord and Saviour already. (Acts 2:36.)

Here's another excerpt from my article.

'Works Salvationists want people to go to hell.

Think about it. They've condemned gays, porn addicts, backsliders, alcoholics, and loose-living people; obviously they want these people to go to hell. There's no grace in their theology! None! Demanding people to live a certain way when they know they can't. Romans 7:18. I hate to be so harsh, but you Works Salvationists, and you know exactly who you are, are a blight to the gospel of grace and a poison to Christianity. The Bible condemns you! (1 Corinthians 11:32.)

I do not apologize for writing the article that this except was extracted from because Lordship Salvation does nothing but cause spiritual rebellion! I do apologize to those, who out of ignorance or bad preaching, believe such heresies but don't want to believe them. In fact, this was written for your readership.

What is the basis of Lordship salvation?

They use Matthew 7:22–23 and claim that the will of God is to obey the law.

Matthew 7:22–23 — *Many will say to me in that day, Lord, Lord, have we not prophesied in thy name? and in thy name have cast out devils? and in thy name done many wonderful works? And then will I profess unto them, I never knew you: depart from me, ye that work iniquity.*

This verse is probably the most abused verse in the New Testament when it comes to doctrine. Lordship Salvationists make it their hallmark verse. Straight is the gate and narrow is the way, they quote and with that understanding of scripture they lay a foundation for the constitution of this foolish doctrine. If straight is the gate and the Christian walk is narrow then they must make the gospel difficult by saying, "true believers" will make Christ the Lord of their life. That's not what John 3:16 or any of the other Sola Fide scriptures say.

The gospel is to believe in/on Jesus Christ for salvation. Nowhere in scripture does it say that you must make Christ the Lord of your life. Acts 16:31, says to believe on the Lord Jesus Christ, not make Christ your Lord. That concept is manipulated into the text by man's self-made doctrines and faulty exegesis. What Matthew 7:22 is saying is that we must do the will of God. Which is true.

Colossians 1:1 — *Paul, an apostle of Jesus Christ through the will of God, and Timotheus the brother.*

They have, however confused the will of God with obedience to the law or good works. A friend of mine said that the will of God was to obey the Ten Commandments. Another person said that no one could know what the will of God was. He condemns himself and others to hell every time he sojourns a church. If obeying the Ten Commandments was the will of God then no one is or can be saved! Not even the apostle Paul for he admitted that he didn't obey the tenth commandment. (Thou shalt not covet.) Everyone covets. (Jeremiah 6:13.)

So what is the will of God?

Lordship theology says good works!

But what does the Bible say.

John 6:28–29 — *They said therefore unto him, 'What may we do that we may work the works of God?' Jesus answered and said to them, 'This is the work of God, that ye may believe in him whom He did send.*

These scriptures confirm that there is only one work that we must do for salvation and that is to believe in Jesus Christ. What does the Bible say the will of God is? Forget about what man says. Forget about what some Lordship Salvationist says. What does the Bible clearly say?

John 6:38–40 — *For I came down from heaven, not to do mine own will, but the will of him that sent me. And this is the Father's will which hath sent me, that of all which he hath given me I should lose nothing, but should raise it up again at the last day. And this is the will of him that sent me, that every one which seeth the Son, and **believeth** on him, may have everlasting life: and I will raise him up at the last day.*

The will of God is for us to have eternal life. We get this by believing in Christ as scripture plainly states.

The Lordship Salvationist uses the latter part of Matthew 7:23 to refer to those who work iniquity as Christians who sin or habitually sin. But all Christians sin: (Ecclesiastes 7:20, Romans 3:23, Psalm 116:11, Galatians 3:22). So what could this be talking about? It's talking about those who tried to work their way to heaven. This includes the Lordship Salvationists who until they decide to trust Christ by simple faith are still lost. When they meet Christ on judgment day they will say: didn't we prophecy, cast out demons and do other wonderful works in your name and Christ will say depart from me I never knew you! This verse refutes Lordship salvation to the chagrin of some Lordship Salvationists who use it to espouse their heresy.

This verse even applies to the Buddhist, the atheist the Muslim who didn't believe in Jesus and instead will brag about their good works. All those who are outside of Christ are workers of iniquities even the humanitarian moralist that incessantly donates to charities. The Bible says that even our good deeds are like filthy rags. (Isaiah 64:6.) There's nothing wrong with doing good deeds as long as you have trusted Christ and Christ alone for salvation. But the line is drawn when good deeds become a prerequisite for salvation.

Here's another excerpt from my article.

A Works Salvationist is an invader among Christians and worthy of the title: spiritual Hitler! There is no Christic love in them. For they want no one to be saved. Imagine someone walking around a church admiring all the children in a Christlike fashion, but in the back of their mind they're thinking that most of them are going to end up in hell because they won't measure up to their legalistic standard. I'm sorry, there is not a scintilla of Christocentric love in someone like that! I thank God that works are not in my soteriology. If there is an evil that goes unseen in Christendom it is works salvation!

Or Lordship Salvation!

Some people reading this may disagree that Lordship Salvationists don't love people. If they truly loved people then why are they making salvation so hard for them? Is that true love? They need to repent from the sin of making salvation difficult!

The will of God is to believe in Jesus for everlasting life.

Lordship Salvation is a lie!

Salvation is a free gift, not a tradeoff or barter. If you had to do something other than believe in order to be saved, as Lordship theology posits then the gift of grace ceases to be a gift! Don't buy into all the Lordship garbage. Easy-Believism is true for there is simplicity in Christ.

2 Corinthians 11:3 — *But I fear, lest by any means, as the serpent beguiled Eve through his subtlety, so your minds should be corrupted from the simplicity that is in Christ.*

Lordship Salvation falls flat on its heretical face in light of Romans 4:5 — *But to him that worketh not, but believeth on him that justifieth the ungodly, his faith is counted for righteousness.*

What does Lordship Salvation produce?

Self-righteousness.

Pride.

Self-confidence.

A distortion of the gospel. (Faith plus works.)

Judgmentalism.

Redefinitions of faith.

(Head faith, heart faith, dead faith, demonic faith, non-saving faith, false faith, spurious faith, efficacious faith, mental assent faith ... whatever.)

Prejudice towards carnal Christians and backsliders.

Bad doctrine.

An impossible standard to live by.

An unknowable standard to live by.

No assurance of salvation.

Rebellion.

Self-defeat.

Accusations of people being false converts.

NO SALVATION!

Anyone who loves Christ and others needs to <u>HATE</u> this damnable doctrine!

Secure In Christ.

And Jesus said unto them, I am the bread of life: he that cometh to me shall never hunger; and he that believeth on me shall never thirst. —
John 6:35.

~ 20 ~

Instantaneous Salvation

Acts 16:29–31 — *Then he called for a light, and sprang in, and came trembling, and fell down before Paul and Silas, And brought them out, and said, Sirs, what must I do to be saved? And they said, Believe on the Lord Jesus Christ, and thou shalt be saved, and thy house.*

The verb "believe" is in the aorist tense. This is what saves someone. The first time a person believes in Christ he is instantly saved. It is not faith (noun) that first saves someone, but believing (verb). Faith (noun) is what a believer is currently undergoing but if this faith (noun) should falter or run out, nothing can negate or change the fact that they first believed (verb).

Ephesians 2:8 describes faith (noun) as what saves us or in this case what gives us a standing in grace.

For by grace are ye saved through faith; and that not of yourselves: it is the gift of God.

Faith and belief are both nouns. It takes a verb to get saved. If salvation is by faith alone (Sola Fide) then it must be a onetime act of faith otherwise it isn't alone for continual faith is an appendage to faith. We are saved by faith alone; not faith plus more faith, plus even more faith. The idea of continual faith for salvation is unbiblical and bereft of reason!

John W. White expounds deeper on this.

123

"Saved is a perfect passive nominative participle used as an adjective to describe the subject, ye, implied by the second person plural of the verb Eijmi. The perfect tense is graphed with a combination of the aorist tense and the present tense, or a (·) and a line (¾) and therefore it would look like this: (¾). The perfect tense expresses the continuance of completed action in the past."

In other words, my salvation continues not because I keep on believing but because Christ died for me and He keeps on believing, this active ongoing belief was established before I was even born, (Titus 1:1–2.) at Calvary and is still interminably active forevermore. Salvation is not finished by our continual belief; it was finished completely at Calvary. Tetelastai. (John 19:30.)

Theologians have estimated that upon salvation a number of things happen to a Christian. L.S. Chafer estimates about forty, some theologians have estimated upwards to about fifty or sixty. But I can give you 12 of the essentials that occur upon instant salvation.

You are regenerated by the Holy Spirit. Titus 3:5.

You are indwelt by the Holy Spirit. John 14:16.

You are baptized into Christ's body. 1 Corinthians 12:12–13.

You are sealed in Christ. Ephesians 1:13.

You are adopted in Christ. Ephesians 1:5.

You are forgiven. Colossians 2:13.

You are justified. Romans 5:1.

You are reconciled. 2 Corinthians 5:19.

You are redeemed. Ephesians 1:7.

You are given everlasting life. Romans 6:23.

You are guaranteed future glorification. Romans 8:18–23.

You are sanctified. Acts 20:32.

* * *

The tenses of salvation.

Past (Luke 7:50.)

Justification.

Sin's penalty.

Present. (1 Corinthians 1:18.)

Sanctification.

Sin's power.

Future. (Romans 13:11.)

Glorification.

Sin's presence.

Why don't some people believe that salvation is permanent and instantaneous upon first-time believing?

Well one reason is because it seems too simple. People don't like the idea that all a person has to do is come to Christ in order to be saved. That's not fair. They can live any way they want and still be saved. Yepp! The reason people don't like this notion nor do they understand it is because they fail to understand that once a person is saved and adopted into the body of Christ, (Galatians 4:5) God is not detached, absent and inactive in their lives.

Now the conspicuity of God's inner workings in each believer differs. For instance, God may appear to be absent in a believer's life so that the believer can take some time to learn about the hazards of life. God may wait for the opportune juncture before disciplining individual Christians. God may be doing an invisible work in their lives that others cannot see. God may be hardening their hearts as to bring them to a point of obvious depravity so that they can see themselves more honestly in light of sin. God may be trying to chastise His children and they might be persistently shunning it.

God works in mysterious ways. We can't cognize just how God is working in the lives of His children. I used to think and suffice it to say—that many Christians think—that if a professing believer isn't bearing any fruit and is not chastised by God then they aren't a true believer but once again, we don't know for certain that they aren't bearing fruit and we don't know how God is working in their lives. He may be tarrying as to allow a better opportunity for intervention. The bottom line is we don't know someone's heart and we don't know how God deals with his children.

Another reason people don't understand how salvation can take place in an instant is because there is a myth that Christians are given new natures upon conversion. We as Christians still have the old nature otherwise we wouldn't sin ever. (Romans 8:23.) The Christian is however given the Holy Spirit. (Galatians 4:6.) That is what enables us to vie against sin and temptation. Putting off the old man doesn't mean you have gotten rid of the old nature. It simply means that the carnal nature that lost people possess doesn't have to take full dominion over your behavior. And it is true that addicts have to give in to their addictions until treatment is implemented, but even someone who compulsively smokes doesn't have to do so every second of every day.

The problem with most people's theology is that they think that Christians will naturally overcome certain sins due to the indwelling of the Holy Spirit. This is not true. Without proper training and spiritual growth, no such victory over sin is possible and even still it is something the Christian must diligently work at by employing the power of the Holy Spirit through prayer, scripture reading and memorizing, counseling or whatever.

The reason so many Christians are disillusioned is because when they came to Christ they had virtually no known habits so they feel as if that's what it means to be Christians. You can sin occasionally, just not habitually, they think. With others, they get delivered from a sin that was destroying their marriage for example and then they falsely presuppose that all Christians go through the exact same deliverance experience. It would be as silly for me to think that now that I'm a Christian I automatically have the power to overcome smoking. I'm an overcomer. When the truth is; I've never smoked!

People need to realize that those who have spent years—even decades trapped in multiple addictions and carnality and then get saved have more problematic baggage than the average church-grown Christian that was never exposed to all the throes, plights and vices of this evil world. The idea that Christians, "true Christians" if you will, live by a certain standard, one in which man has conceived based on his own opinion is unbiblical and thus swamped in pride and intolerance for human weakness.

"Putting off the old man" doesn't mean, saying goodbye to the old nature.

Colossians 3:9 — *Lie not one to another, seeing that ye have put off the old man with his deeds.*

If the old nature were gone then why would Paul be encouraging his people to not lie to one another? It makes no sense to tell someone to do something if they don't have the causative nature to do what it is you're telling them not to do.

Of course we have the ability to lie, and cuss and commit all sorts of other heinous sins—even as Christians. Why, because we still have the old nature in full bloom. It hasn't changed, lessoned, reduced, deintensified, curbed, suppressed or minimized in anyway. The difference however between Christians and non-Christians is that we have the Holy Spirit. If a Christian says no to sin and yes to holiness it is only because of the Holy Spirit.

Romans 7:20 — *Now if I do that I would not, it is no more I that do it, but sin that dwelleth in me.*

The "sin that dwelleth in me," is the old nature. Hamartia oikeo en emoi. In Greek means: "sin that remains fixed in my property."

So, yes, we do still have the same old nature as we did when we were children of the devil. There will be people that deny this—thinking that they do have a new nature and even deny or partially deny the reality of the immanent old nature. Well read this verse.

Job 9:20 — *If I justify myself, mine own mouth shall condemn me: if I say, I am perfect, it shall also prove me perverse.*

The word 'perfect' here is used to express moral uprightness not sinless perfection. This applies to those who piously tout their own morality. Their own mouth condemns them.

For anyone that believes that our old nature is transformed by or into a new nature, they must answer these three questions.

If our old nature is made new, then why isn't it perfect?

If our old nature is made new then why do we need the Holy Spirit? (1 Corinthians 3:16.)

If our old nature is made new, then why are we not in heaven now?

The bottom line is that if salvation isn't received by one act of simple faith then nobody can be saved and furthermore nobody can know that they are saved here and now. Read again the chapter entitled: Assurance Of Salvation for more insight on this subject.

I entitled this chapter 'instantaneous salvation' so it behooves me give a few scriptures that explain this doctrine.

Ephesians 1:13 — *In whom ye also trusted, after that ye heard the word of truth, the gospel of your salvation: in whom also after that ye believed, ye were sealed with that holy Spirit of promise.*

The moment you believe you are instantaneously sealed!

The NLT reads: And when you believed in Christ, he identified you as his own.

The sealing of the Holy Spirit and believing for salvation happened simultaneously!

That's instantaneous salvation.

Praise God!

If eternity starts <u>now</u> and goes on <u>forever</u> then it has to be given to us instantaneously!

Ephesians 2:13 — *But <u>now</u> in Christ Jesus ye who sometimes were far off are made nigh by the blood of Christ.*

It says that you are made nigh to Christ by the blood. "Now" denotes the instantaneousness of salvation.

John 5:24–25 — *Verily, verily, I say unto you, He that heareth my word, and believeth on him that sent me, hath everlasting life, and shall not come into condemnation; but is passed from death unto life. Verily, verily, I say unto you, The hour is coming, and now is, when the dead shall hear the voice of the Son of God: and they that hear shall live.*

Verse 24 is obvious that the very instantaneous moment we believe on Christ we will have eternal life but look at verse 25. Now is when the hearing of the voice of the son of God is taking place, not later, and the promise to all those who hear is: and they that hear shall live ... that's eternal life that comes in an instant.

1 John 3:2 — *Beloved, <u>now</u> are we the sons of God, and it doth not yet appear what we shall be: but we know that, when he shall appear, we shall be like him; for we shall see him as he is.*

This verse says that we are sons of God right now. The only way this promise could be true is if the sonship through rebirth happens in an instant. Right now, instantaneously!

Secure In Christ.

~ 21 ~

Roman Road Revised

The Roman road to salvation works in winning souls to Christ. It is a crafty and popular way to show people the gospel by traveling through the book of Romans. The scriptures are in this order: 3:23, 5:8–9, 6–23, 10:9–10, 10:13.

This works and is fine but due to the usage of "confession," this might not be the best approach to go by. Someone might distort the meaning of confession to public confession or corporate confession. The witnesser may scare the witnessee due to shyness or lack of oratorical skills.

Confession is even a work. It takes vocal work. Let's say a person has strep throat or a cold and they can hardly produce any vocables. Confession for them would take work.

And salvation is not by works (Titus 3:5. Galatians 2:16, 3:11, 2 Timothy 1:9).

Is confession even part of salvation ... or proof of salvation?

What is the point of confession?
Romans 10:9 — *That if thou shalt confess with thy mouth the Lord Jesus, and shalt believe in thine heart that God hath raised him from the dead, thou shalt be saved.*

Confession is not a condition of salvation, neither is it proof. It is simply an act of obedience. I encourage it but we should not embarrass the person we are witnessing to by making them verbalize their belief in Christ. God knows their heart. If the person is willing to confess then go for it. In this Romanic context the confession results in physical or temporal salvation. Eternal salvation is only conditioned on believing.

Romans 10:10 — *For with the heart man believeth unto righteousness; and with the mouth confession is made unto salvation.*

Some say that you must believe with the heart and then subsequently confess as if both the verbal confession and the believing in the heart were synergistically necessary. The confession is not a part of eternal salvation otherwise mute, deaf or shy people couldn't be saved. Believing in Christ is what saves a person and it comes prior to the confession.

Confession is not a separate action that accompanies salvation. Confession may confirm that the person has believed, but it is not part of it. Romans 10:13, says that if you call upon the name of the Lord you shall be saved. See also Acts 2:21.

Romans 10:13 — *For whosoever shall call upon the name of the Lord shall be saved.*

But Romans 10:14 says that such a call is not possible unless it is preceded by believing.

Romans 10:14 — *How then shall they call on him in whom they have not believed? and how shall they believe in him of whom they have not heard? and how shall they hear without a preacher?*

What's the point? The point is for one to be saved he must desire to be saved. Someone said that if my message, (this book) which the Bible clearly supports, were true then everyone would be saved. What she was implying was that if grace were truly free and faith in Christ were the only means of salvation then the whole world could be saved. According to this lady, Salvation must be more difficult so that only few people can have it. This is works salvation! This lady obviously didn't want sinful people to be saved. How Christless!

The Bible is clear that God wants all people to be saved and He makes it as easy as can be. The reason all people won't be saved is because they don't want salvation. A free gift only benefits the recipient if he receives the gift. Nevertheless, God wants all to be saved.

2 Peter 3:9 — *The Lord is not slack concerning his promise, as some men count slackness; but is longsuffering to us-ward, not willing that any should perish, but that all should come to repentance.*

Faith in Christ is pretty simple. Man makes it difficult because of inherent pride.

The old Romans Road message works, but we should consider the new Romans Road as well. In this order.

The revised Romans Road is this.

Romans 3:10, 23.

Romans 6:23.

Romans 5:8.

Romans 5:1–2.

John 3:16.

1 John 5:13.

Therefore we conclude that a man is justified by faith without the deeds of the law. —
Romans 3:28.

~ 22 ~

The Doctrines of Justification and Sanctification

For centuries, these two doctrines, because of misconception, have done nothing but sour the good news of the gospel. It's amazing how two pentasyllabic words, misunderstood, taken out of their context, can cause so much doctrinal confusion in Christendom. I have elucidated what these two words actually mean.

Justification. (Dikaiosis.)

Sanctification. (Hagiasmos.)

How do they differ and how do they work together?

Since this is a book on expositional and exegetical theology, I felt it fair and befitting to give only theological definitions to such words.

Justified. (Theology.) To declare innocent or guiltless; absolve; acquit.

Isaiah 43:26 — *Put me in remembrance: let us plead together: declare thou, that thou mayest be justified.*

Sanctified. (Theology.) To make holy; set apart as sacred; consecrate.

1 Chronicles 15:14 — *So the priests and the Levites sanctified themselves to bring up the ark of the LORD God of Israel.*

<u>Justification</u> is a one-time, declarative event. A declaration is not continual, serial, repetitive, progressive or dependent upon any future event or action. It is a decisive act with an uncompromising punctuation!

<u>Sanctification</u> is a continual event, to make holy. Making something takes time and in the Christian's experience of sanctification, it takes the entirety of his or her life.

If these two doctrines are confused or conceptually interfused, then you have allowed your theology to become a rotten egg ready to be dropped!

Look at Hebrews 10:14. (NKJV).

This is a good verse to memorize because therein contains both the concept of justification and sanctification.

Hebrews 10:14 — *For by one offering He has perfected forever those who are being sanctified.*

Let's break this verse apart and hermeneutically dissect its meaning.

"For by one offering," that is referring to Christ's redemptive death on the cross. He, Christ, has perfected forever those, (the sinners, us,) who are <u>being</u> sanctified. (Or being made holy. NIV)

Take a look at the words: "perfected forever." That means that our salvation is complete by a declaration of justification. Christ would have to die again otherwise.

Now look at the words: "being sanctified".

This has nothing to do with our salvation, it has to do with the continual work Christ is doing in us. This is a lifelong process.

So we have been justified the very moment we believe in Christ.

Acts 13:39 — *And by him all that <u>believe</u> are <u>justified</u> from all things, from which ye could not be <u>justified</u> by the Law of Moses.*

Our cleansing process (sanctification) is forever active thanks to the Holy Spirit dwelling and working within us.

Let's be smart about this.

Justification ... happened once and for all!

Sanctification ... is still happening and won't stop happening until you're dead. However, the process can be interrupted and even terminated by carnality.

These two doctrines wedded together properly explain why man does not stop sinning in this lifetime and also assures us that our good standing with God is only because we've been justified by Christ's work at Calvary.

On judgment day, God will be looking through us as if we have fiber optic bodies. If we've received Christ as our Saviour through faith alone (Sola Fide), then God will see Christ within us. That effulgence of divine holiness alone will blind God from seeing ALL OUR SINS, past, present, and future. This is what guarantees us a ticket into heaven!

Justification gets us into heaven!

Sanctification determines our rewards!

Sola Fide.

But the hour cometh, and now is, when the true worshippers shall worship the Father in spirit and in truth: for the Father seeketh such to worship him. — John 4:23.

~ 23 ~

Salvation Is NOW!

(NLT)

Ephesians 2:5 — *Made us alive with Christ even when we were dead in transgressions—it is by grace you have been saved.*

John 15:3 — *You have already been pruned and purified by the message I have given you.*

Romans 6:5 — *Since we have been united with him in his death, we will also be raised to life as he was.*

Please note: They all say "have been," not will be! So many people will say that we can't be sure of salvation until we pass from this life unto the next. If that were the case, then works would be necessary in knowing if we will enter heaven. And nobody could know this until they've given up the ghost. This is unbiblical. Because if we had to wait and see if we will enter heaven posthumously, we'd never know if we've done enough or have been faithful enough to make it to heaven.

Scripture says:

2 Corinthians 6:2 — *For he saith, I have heard thee in a time accepted, and in the day of salvation have I succoured thee: behold, now is the accepted time; behold, now is the day of salvation.*

It doesn't say: now is the day of getting a provisional salvation started.

139

No. It declares that you have received salvation, in full, at that very moment of time.

The idea that we don't have salvation now and can't know if we will have it after this life is absurd. Details granting such assurance that we can only be saved after this life, are biblically unspecific.

Scripture says:

1 Corinthians 1:6–8 — *Even as the testimony of Christ was confirmed in you: So that ye come behind in no gift; waiting for the coming of our Lord Jesus Christ: Who shall also confirm you* <u>*unto the end*</u>*, that ye may be blameless in the day of our Lord Jesus Christ.*

Jesus not only confirms that we are saved, but he does it at the moment of faith and continues to confirm this until we die.

The scripture doesn't say:

Who shall also confirm you <u>in the end</u>, that ye may be blameless in the day of our Lord Jesus Christ.

Read it again; it says:

Who shall also confirm you <u>unto the end</u>.

"Unto" means from now until the end.

So if you are saved now, then your salvation is secure from now on, upwards unto the moment you will be with Christ in heaven.

What about if we don't maintain good works in this life?

To answer this is simple.

Nobody maintains enough good deeds in this lifetime to be good enough to merit heaven on their own.

Read the following Pauline words.

Philippians 3:12 — *Not as though I had already attained, either were already perfect: but I follow after, if that I may apprehend that for which also I am apprehended of Christ Jesus.*

When Paul writes: "not as though I had already attained," he is referring to his own state of righteousness or worthiness. It is Christ's righteousness that declares us saved. He is admitting that he has yet to attain such a completed holy state in his current lifetime.

Take a look at the following verses.

Colossians 3:1–4 — *If ye then be risen with Christ, seek those things which are above, where Christ sitteth on the right hand of God.*

Risen with Christ excludes the idea of not permanently having salvation at the moment of faith. This is pretty strong language denoting that we have salvation instantaneously now; otherwise it couldn't say that we were sitting with Christ at the right-hand of God. Nor would it tell us to seek those things, which are above. We seek now in this lifetime because we've already attained salvation through faith.

Set your affection on things above, not on things on the earth.

This is saying that we have salvation, so we should set our affection or predilection on heavenly things.

For ye are dead, and your life is hid with Christ in God.

We are dead in Christ and hidden in Him. How could we not have salvation now if we are hidden with Him? This makes me cogitate about being surgically implanted into our Saviour. How on earth can anything we do in this life prescind us from such an eternally secured position?

When Christ, who is our life, shall appear, then shall ye also appear with him in glory.

Of course salvation is ours the moment we come to Christ in faith alone otherwise this verse would not suggest that we would appear with Him in glory—which means in heaven!

The idea that salvation is given to us but is not fully attained right here and now and or can be lost in any capacity suggests that it is up to us to keep ourselves saved.

This implies that God can't independently save us and furthermore implies that He can't keep us saved!

Scripture refutes this!

Once saved, we are His possessions, His children.

God's faithfulness is what guarantees that we have salvation the moment we believe in Christ.

1 Corinthians 1:9 — *God is faithful, by whom ye were called unto the fellowship of his Son Jesus Christ our Lord.*

Here are some more verses.

Romans 5:11 — *And not only so, but we also joy in God through our Lord Jesus Christ, by whom we have <u>now</u> received the atonement.*

If we've received the atonement now, than suffice it to say that salvation is also given to us now.

Philippians 3:20 — *For our conversation is in heaven; from whence also we look for the Saviour, the Lord Jesus Christ.*

Conversation is another word for citizenship. This verse is saying that our citizenship is now in heaven. For this not to be true, it would have to read: for our conversation (citizenship) will be in heaven. It says that it is (present-active) in heaven.

So if you have trusted in Christ to be your Saviour, you have eternal life already!

And this truth is also verified antithetically.

Those who are not in Christ have already been judged.

John 3:18 (NLT) — *There is no judgment against anyone who believes in him. But anyone who does not believe in him <u>has already been judged</u> for not believing in God's one and only Son.*

By this evidence, we can be certain that the good news of the gospel promises salvation NOW!

Sola Fide.

For we must all appear before the judgment seat of Christ; that every one may receive the things done in his body, according to that he hath done, whether it be good or bad. — 2 Corinthians 5:10.

~ 24 ~

Books of Life

The Solafidian doctrine is often marred and abused by scriptures in the Book of Revelation that speak of having names blotted out of the book of life.

I hope the following thesis will elucidate my case and clear up the misunderstood rumors about these verses.

Luke 10:20 — *Notwithstanding in this rejoice not, that the spirits are subject unto you; but rather rejoice, because your names are written in heaven.*

Luke had assurance of his salvation. Otherwise he couldn't say that his name was written in heaven.

If his assurance wavered or stood on sinking sand, he might have said something to the effect of: because your names might be written in heaven someday if you qualify.

Other scriptures refer to the Lamb's book of life.

Revelation 21:27 — *And there shall in no wise enter into it any thing that defileth, neither whatsoever worketh abomination, or maketh a lie: but they which are written in the Lamb's book of life.*

There are only 3 verses in the Bible where: "Lamb's book of life" is mentioned.

The others are Revelation 13:8, v 21:27.

We'll get there.

The following verses are concerning the book of life.

There are other allusive references to having names written in and blotted out of books. Exodus 32:32–33 are examples. However this thesis is on the "books of life", so I will now only deal with such germane verses.

Philippians 4:3 — *And I intreat thee also, true yokefellow, help those women which <u>laboured</u> with me in the gospel, with Clement also, and with other my <u>fellow labourers</u>, whose names are in the book of life.*

The book of life is a record of works for rewards.

Revelation 3:5 — *He that overcometh, the same shall be clothed in white raiment; and I will not blot out his name out of the book of life, but I will confess his name before my Father, and before his angels.*

"Overcometh" denotes a Christian who diligently endured to the end. His name won't be blotted out of the book of life, evoking that he will receive abundant rewards.

An overcomer is not someone who is sinless, just someone who confessed his sins routinely and fought the good fight of faith to the end.

Revelation 13:8 — *And all that dwell upon the earth shall worship him, whose names are not written in the book of life of the Lamb slain from the foundation of the world.*

This is referring to people worshipping the antichrist. If you read the "before" and "after" verses you will know that this is not referring to people worshipping God. The KJV isn't clear on this verse if read in isolation. But the NLT uses the term "worship the beast" so that you know that the people whose names are not written in the Lamb's book of life are worshipping Satan and not Jehovah God.

Revelation 21:27 — *And there shall in no wise enter into it any thing that defileth, neither whatsoever worketh abomination, or maketh a lie: but they which are written in the Lamb's book of life.*

This is referring to born-again Christians as being the only enterers into heaven because their names were written in the Lamb's book of life. The point is that there are two books.

Revelation 20:12 — *And I saw the dead, small and great, stand before God; and the books were opened: and another book was opened, which is the book of life: and the dead were judged out of those things which were written in the books, according to their works.*

The Lamb's book of life is the book that Christian's names are written in at the moment of salvation through faith alone in Christ alone.

The "book of life" is a book that will be used only to judge works. If you are saved, your works will be judged by this book, which contains therein all your deeds—good or bad. If you are lost, likewise will happen. But the thing to remember is that the only things lost people have in the end is there futile works. So they will be judged based on the recordings from the same book.

Revelation 17:8 — *The beast that thou sawest was, and is not; and shall ascend out of the bottomless pit, and go into perdition: and they that dwell on the earth shall wonder, whose names were not written in the book of life from the foundation of the world, when they behold the beast that was, and is not, and yet is.*

Revelation 22:19 — *And if any man shall take away from the words of the book of this prophecy, God shall take away his part out of the book of life, and out of the holy city, and from the things which are written in this book.*

Having your part taken away from the book of life is not having your salvation taken away; it is referring to rewards. Part in Greek is meros, meaning lot or inheritance. That is the consequence to disobedience and in this case taking away words from the Bible or committing heresy.

What about this final verse about the books of life.

Revelation 20:15 — *And whosoever was not found written in the book of life was cast into the lake of fire.*

This is a final judgment verse that is pertaining to the lost. Back it up to verse 20:11 and you will see that this is the great white throne judgment. That is the judgment seat of the lost exclusively. If a person is lost, his name surely isn't written in the Lamb's book of life so, that is why this book is being opened and scrutinized. Why is a lost person's name not even written in the book of life? Because this is a book that records deeds, works, sins, and lawlessness. Even a lost person's good deeds mean nothing to God.

Hebrews 11:16 — *But <u>without faith</u> it is impossible to please him: for he that cometh to God must believe that he is, and that he is a rewarder of them that diligently seek him.*

Back to the thesis.

Christians are given new names because they are given eternal life. The lost, in their cesspool of sins and wickedness, didn't want to receive a new life or a new name for that matter, hence explaining why their names were not recorded in the Lamb's book of life.

That's the difference between the two books.

I believe that a Christian's name is in both books.

One for salvation: (Lamb's book of life.)

And the other for rewards: (book of life.)

Philippians 4:3 — *And I intreat thee also, true yokefellow, help those women which laboured with me in the gospel, with Clement also, and with other my fellow labourers, whose <u>names are in the book of life</u>.*

This is just one interpretation of the name-blotted-out doctrine.

There are others that don't go gainsay with Sola fide.

For instance.

Some believe John is exhorting with a promise to the believers in Revelation 3:5. The Christian, who is automatically an overcomer, (1 John 5:5) is already written in God's book of Life, the record of all of God's elect unto salvation. Contrary to how human societies would remove a dissident from the city archives so that he or she could no longer reap the benefits of citizenship and is furthermore expulsed, God's promise to His people is that no one, no matter who they are or what they may do, will ever be blotted out of the book of Life. This is the principle of litotes, where the negative affirms the positive. I.e., "I will never hate my girlfriend." This antithetically affirms that I will always love her. It doesn't suggest that hatred is possible. I will never blot out their names. It doesn't mean that there's a chance that their names can be blotted out. Revelation 3:5 according to this view, is a promise of eternal security to God's elect, not a threat of condemnation for not remaining faithful.

I've espoused two viewpoints regarding this subject. Either way you look at it, the idea of losing salvation is not possible as emphasized in other chapters. That would contradict dozens of scriptures. John 3:16. John 3:36. John 5:24. John 6:47. John 10:27–29. Romans 11:29. John 6:37. Romans 8:38–39. Hebrews 7:25. Romans 8:1. Ephesians 4:30. Isaiah 32:17.

God-bless!

But seek ye first the kingdom of God, and his righteousness; and all these things shall be added unto you. — Matthew 6:33.

~ 25 ~

Imputed Righteousness

Imputed righteousness is the righteousness of God imputed to us the moment we believe in Christ for salvation. It is not our own righteousness, (Philippians 3:9, Isaiah 64:6) but the perfect righteousness of Christ. "Impute" means to account or credit to.

Philemon. 1:18 — *If he hath wronged thee, or oweth thee ought, put that on mine account.*

Imagine a judge writing your name on a pardon. He declares you "not guilty." He doesn't make you "not guilty." He simply declares this verdict. Imputed righteousness is God's righteousness bestowed to man upon faith.

Romans 10:3 — *For they being ignorant of God's righteousness, and going about to establish their own righteousness, have not submitted themselves unto the righteousness of God.*

Those who deny the doctrine of imputation are guilty of doing what those in this verse are doing—establishing their own self-righteousness.

In Genesis, Abraham demonstrates imputed righteousness.

Genesis 15:6 — *And he believed in the LORD; and he counted it to him for righteousness.*

His initial act of believing in God was how God's righteousness was accounted unto him. Abraham, like all men, was still in his own experience a sinner. But it was God's imputed righteousness that granted him salvation.

Romans 4:11 — *And he received the sign of circumcision, a seal of the righteousness of the faith which he had yet being uncircumcised: that he might be the father of all them that believe, though they be not circumcised; that righteousness might be imputed unto them also.*

Anyone who believes in Christ for salvation has the very righteousness of Christ. The idea is that of putting on righteousness like a shirt. Underneath this perfect righteousness is still our filthy-rag sin nature. But God, because of Christ's blood, no longer sees our old nature.

Joshua demonstrates this.

Zechariah 3:2–4 — *And the LORD said unto Satan, The LORD rebuke thee, O Satan; even the LORD that hath chosen Jerusalem rebuke thee: is not this a brand plucked out of the fire? Now Joshua was clothed with filthy garments, and stood before the angel. And he answered and spake unto those that stood before him, saying, Take away the filthy garments from him. And unto him he said, Behold, I have caused thine iniquity to pass from thee, and I will clothe thee with change of raiment.*

This metaphorically illustrates imputed righteousness. The change of raiment represents God's pure righteousness being securely placed upon the sinner.

Isaiah 61:10 — *I will greatly rejoice in the LORD, my soul shall be joyful in my God; for he hath clothed me with the garments of salvation, he hath covered me with the robe of righteousness, as a bridegroom decketh himself with ornaments, and as a bride adorneth herself with her jewels.*

Key phrase: "Robe of righteousness." This makes it clear that it is not our own righteousness that saves us—thank God! It is His righteousness that is imputed unto us upon belief in Christ.

Romans 4:22–24 — *And therefore it was <u>imputed</u> to him for righteousness. Now it was not written for his sake alone, that it* *was underlined to him; But for us also, to whom it shall be imputed, if we believe on him that raised up Jesus our Lord from the dead.*

Romans 4:6–8 — *Even as David also describeth the blessedness of the man, unto whom God imputeth righteousness without works, Saying, Blessed are they whose iniquities are forgiven, and whose sins are covered. Blessed is the man to whom the Lord will not impute sin.*

Imputation is Christ swapping places with the sinner.

He was perfect or ... just. Deuteronomy 32:4.

We are sinful and ... unjust. Galatians 3:22.

1 Peter 3:18 — *For Christ also hath once suffered for sins, the just for the unjust, that he might bring us to God, being put to death in the flesh, but quickened by the Spirit.*

Some people refuse this biblical truth, but that is because they are trying to establish their own righteousness, which is by the law.

Philippians 3:9 — *And be found in him, not having mine own righteousness, which is of the law, but that which is through the faith of Christ, the righteousness which is of God by faith.*

Trying to obey the law cannot save because obeying the law cannot save. Salvation comes only by faith in Christ. (John 3:16; Ephesians 2:8–9; and Luke 7:50.)

Romans 3:27 — *Where is boasting then? It is excluded. By what law? of works? Nay: but by the law of faith.*

We need God's righteousness to be saved.

We get it by faith or believing in Christ.

James 2:23 — *And the scripture was fulfilled which saith, Abraham believed God, and it was imputed unto him for righteousness: and he was called the Friend of God.*

Not only will God impute His righteousness to us, (believers.) But He will also NOT impute our sins to us.

2 Corinthians 5:19 — *To wit, that God was in Christ, reconciling the world unto himself, <u>not imputing</u> their trespasses unto them; and hath committed unto us the word of reconciliation.*

Psalm 32:1–2 — *Blessed is he whose transgression is forgiven, whose sin is covered. Blessed is the man unto whom the LORD imputeth not iniquity, and in whose spirit there is no guile.*

Imputed righteousness needs to be understood if we are to fully understand God's greatness and love. In Adam, sin was imputed to every person. Romans 5:12. But in Christ, eternal life is offered to all men. Romans 5:15.

Righteousness, which is essential to entrance in heaven, is only attained by faith alone in Christ. Trying to obey the law in order to be saved and sadly many are in this camp, is silly and futile and won't save anyone!

Galatians 2:21 — *I do not frustrate the grace of God: for if righteousness come by the law, then Christ is dead in vain.*

Righteousness cannot come by the law for the law cannot perfect anybody. Hebrews 10:1.

Righteousness can only come by faith alone in Christ. Romans 10:10 makes this crystal clear.

Romans 10:10 — *For with the heart man believeth unto righteousness; and with the mouth confession is made unto salvation.*

Imputed righteousness is simply God giving us—sinful creatures—the righteousness of His very son.

2 Corinthians 5:21 — *For he hath made him to be sin for us, who knew no sin; that we might be made the <u>righteousness of God</u> in him.*

Faith needs no work.

How then can man be justified with God? or how can he be clean that is born of a woman? — Job 25:4.

~ 26 ~

The Gospel According To The Smurfs

In the first season of the Smurfs, episode 31, entitled: "Smurfette," is aptly illustrated the biblical doctrine of justification. Gargamel, basking in perpetual misery, decided that he was sick of the laughter and felicity that the Smurf community exhibited. He felt the inner need to arouse some confusion.

The perfect plan that every evil genius knew that would get the Smurfs attention was to create a she-Smurf, ... a Smurfette. He created her out of blue clay and other such wizardry ingredients. She ended up being black-haired and plain-dressed but nevertheless blandly feminine.

During a Smurf-berry pick, a Smurf arbitrarily found her lost in the woods crying: "Boo-hoo-hoo, I'm all alone and have nowhere to go."

The Smurf, (and I can't remember which one) escorts her to Papa Smurf and the rest of the Smurf village. The Smurfs don't know what to think of her. She dances around seductively, showing off her girliness and the male Smurfs react baffled more so than aroused. She even asked Handy Smurf something to the effect of:

"What are you waiting on? Aren't you going to carry me?"

He stood quizzical for a moment and the whole scenario ended up with him throwing her over his shoulders like a sac of potatoes whereas she was expecting to be heroically cradled in his arms.

Later in the episode, Gargamel consulted with her through her magical mirror and instructed her to bring the Smurf village to ruins. She tried to and succeeded in coaxing a Smurf into releasing the floodwater from the dam in order to flood the Smurf village.

She was found guilty and ordered to a tribunal where Papa Smurf was the judge. With no hesitation, she cried, admitting that Gargamel created her and now she wanted to become a real Smurf.

Papa Smurf ungrudgingly took her into his lab and whipped up a transformative concoction. It instantly morphed her into a delightful, blond-haired, blue-eyed she-Smurf with a white flowery dress.

This is the doctrine of justification. Christ doesn't give you the ability to justify yourself; he transforms you in one instantaneous act due to our belief in Him. (Luke 7:50)

All the Smurfs, upon Smurfette's conversion oohed and awhhed as if they finally understood why it was they were supposed to like her. They fought over her for she was now a real Smurf.

This is the gospel. The fact that Gargamel created Smurfette is proof that her nature, in origin, was defiled. Because of this wretched nature, she tried to flood the Smurf village. Guilty was her verdict! But what did Papa Smurf do for her? He forgave her and gave her a chance to be redeemed. Her new body typifies her new nature that was made perfect or "Smurfect" if you will only because of what Papa Smurf did in his lab.

This is what happens when we admit that we are a sinner to Christ and place simple faith in Him. We get a new nature by position, which is the only way we may receive eternal life in heaven.

<u>Faith alone in Christ alone.</u>

Secure In Christ.

*Come now, and let us reason together, saith the
LORD: though your sins be as scarlet, they shall
be as white as snow; though they be red like
crimson, they shall be as wool.* — Isaiah 1:18.

~ 27 ~

The Color of Salvation

Isaiah 1:18 — *Come now, and let us reason together, saith the LORD: though your sins be as scarlet, they shall be as white as snow; though they be red like crimson, they shall be as wool.*

Why can't we save ourselves? Why can't we commune with God without our fellowship through Christ? It's simple. Let's color our sins. Now let's set a precedent of <u>total</u> <u>sinlessness</u> and color it red. Pure deep, crimson red. The color of Christ's shed blood!

Everybody else who sins is a color branded by their sin. We all know that red, yellow and blue are primary colors; immiscible in effect to make other colors or illegitimate nuances of the original color, but unable to be perfected by secondary colors.

In other words, red is red, blue is blue and all primary colors are unalloyed.

Why don't sins have degrees? Note. I'm not talking about consequences; I'm talking about the sin itself.

Sins don't have degrees because compared to righteousness (Christ) they are still no-good, misbegotten and far from red. The color orange will never be red. You can't make red no matter how hard you try. So we as humans can't be right with God unless He makes us right through Christ. Our own volitional works would approximate "blending colors" in attempt to make red. Is hot-pink, red? No. What about orange-red, mahogany, mauve or burnt-sienna?

No matter how close you come to red, you can never become red without Red's help. And it doesn't just help, it replaces! Some people think that after you accept Christ, he will help you become righteous, that's like adding red to brown in hope that the red will superimpose the brown. You can't chromatically annex color to color, you must totally replace the color and that's what Christ does upon our faith in Him. He justifies! We become red because He and He alone is the only true shade of red.

Christians that try to earn their salvation by works or rituals have discolored the pure redness. Works are good as an ancillary action to our acceptance but they don't supplant or compose our acceptance. If you are trying to make works commensurate with acceptance, you've added color.

Let's say that a good deed is white and that self-righteousness is yellow. When you add white to red, what do you get? Pink, right. When you add yellow you get orange. So works held to be tantamount to grace is an ineffectual, counterproductive nonentity.

Don't get me wrong, acts, such as: repentance, the prayer of salvation, baptism, they don't save a person, only Jesus' blood saves a person. The acts however accompany salvation as symbolisms. So Christians should stop trying to pigeonhole sin. Venial sins may be red with a dash of purple or heliotrope with a dash of lilac or cobalt, whereas abominable sins may be a putrid greenish brown in comparison to red, but even a slightly muddled scarlet isn't the true RED!

The redness of Christ makes our filthy sins as white as snow.

This was an amphigory written over two years ago.

God bless!

Faith In Christ Is Eternal Life!

Addendum

Salvation (eternal life) is freely given to anyone who wants it by simply believing that Christ died for his or her sins and that He offers this gift to anyone who will believe in Him for it.

When I took Arianna to the park over a year ago; I discovered the awesomeness of God's love. She would periodically wander away from me and although I would let her go somewhat astray within my scope margin, I was compelled to—by love—follow her and bring her back to me.

This, God does to everyone of his children. That's true agape love. That's free grace. That's eternal joy! That's why I entitled this book: Faith In Christ Is Eternal Life.

JESUS

A

V

E

S

www.ingramcontent.com/pod-product-compliance
Lightning Source LLC
LaVergne TN
LVHW021454080426
835509LV00018B/2280